POCKET

ABU DHABI

TOP SIGHTS • LOCAL EXPERIENCES

JESSICA LEE

Contents

Plan Your Trip 4

Sheikh Zayed Grand Mosque (p104)

Explore Abu Dhabi 28

Worth a Trip

Survival Guide 142

Special Features

Welcome to Abu Dhabi

Proudly modern and cosmopolitan, this dynamic young capital seems to have ants in its pants with its rate of development. Swaths of beach and theme park thrills add family-friendly fun while the Sheikh Zayed Grand Mosque's jaw-dropping architecture and the new Louvre Abu Dhabi's globe-trotting collection cement the city's reputation as the UAE's forward-thinking cultural heart.

Top Sights

LIZCOUGHLAN/SHUTTERSTOCK ©

Louvre Abu Dhabi

Global heritage under one roof. **p86**

ARCHITECT: YOUSEF ABDELKY. LUCIANO MORTULA - LGM/SHUTTERSTOCK ©

Sheikh Zayed Grand Mosque

Islamic architecture's modern triumph. **p104**

EILEEN_10/SHUTTERSTOCK ©

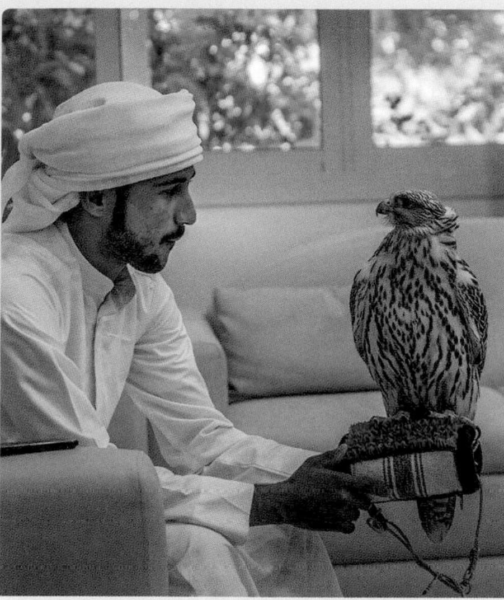

Abu Dhabi Falcon Hospital

Close encounters with Emirati heritage. **p140**

Mangrove National Park

A city-centre nature escape. **p132**

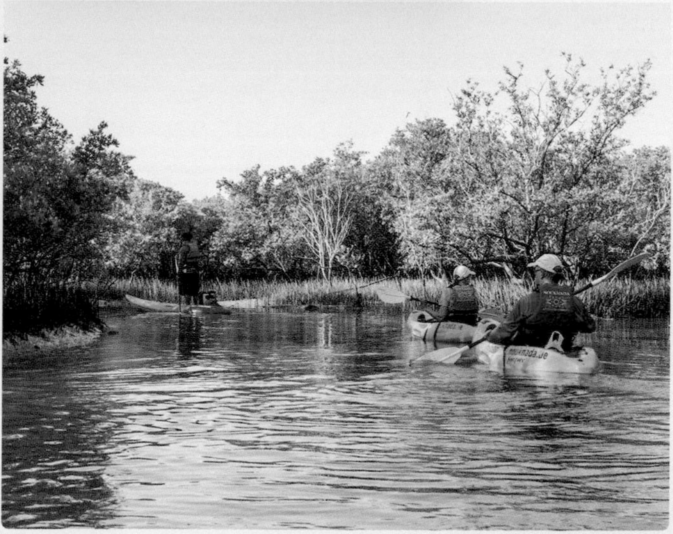

GLEN BERLIN/SHUTTERSTOCK ©

Corniche

An urban playground and promenade. **p32**

MATYAS REHAK/SHUTTERSTOCK ©

LEFT: THE CONSTELLATION BY RALPH HELMICK, FRANKRIS/SHUTTERSTOCK ©; RIGHT: MATYAS REHAK/SHUTTERSTOCK ©

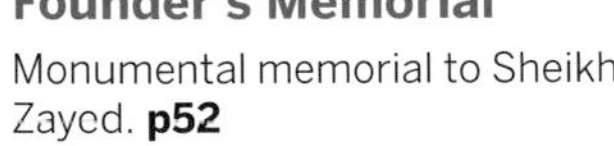

Founder's Memorial

Monumental memorial to Sheikh Zayed. **p52**

Emirates Palace

Get your Gulf glitz on. **p50**

Yas Marina Circuit

World-famous Formula One circuit. p118

Masdar City

A futuristic sustainable city experiment. p120

Abu Dhabi Global Market Square

Modern architecture and a dining hub. p74

Eating

Seafood, Middle Eastern, Indian, Thai and Peruvian. Multicultural Abu Dhabi offers everything from cheap biryanis and eat-on-the-go shawarma to fine dining from across the world. The traditional Gulf dishes of Emirati culture can be more difficult to search out, but there's a handful of options among the wealth of international offerings.

Where to Eat

Abu Dhabi's top fine-dining restaurants tend to be found in the five-star hotels and newer shopping malls. Al Maryah Island is fast becoming one of the major destinations for dining in style. In contrast, the streets one block south of Zayed the First St present a geography of regional cuisine from Syria to Yemen.

What to Eat

Abu Dhabi is a great city for sampling classic Middle Eastern food, despite the fact that it hails from the Levant, not from the Gulf. This usually involves small hot and cold dishes (mezze) such as hummus, *moutabel* (purée of aubergine) and *sambusak* (cheese-filled pastries), which are enjoyed over long chats and with a watermelon juice to aid digestion. This is followed by rice and meat in various preparations with unleavened bread. Dessert is an afterthought.

Best Middle Eastern Flavours

Li Beirut Fine-dining Levantine style. The place to come for mezze. (p62)

Zahrat Lebnan Families flock here for good-value mezze, shawarma and kebab plates. (p40)

Cafeteria Al Liwan Some of the crispiest falafel and creamiest hummus in town. (p39)

Café Arabia The Middle Eastern menu in this villa bounces from Marrakesh to Istanbul. (p137)

Best Traditional Gulf Tastes

Mezlai Emirati cuisine gets a fine-dining makeover in the Emirates Palace. (p62)

Al Fanar Despite the tack-o-rama facade, this place dishes up the best classic Gulf dishes in town. (p111)

VRANGELS/SHUTTERSTOCK ©

Milas Contemporary twists on Emirati flavours. (p111)

Al Dhafra Tuck into traditional stews and seafood dishes amid Middle Eastern decor. (p97)

Best International Dining

Coya Peruvian cuisine with contemporary flourishes. (p79)

Dai Pai Dong All the dim sum a person could want. (p79)

Ushna Dig into the menu of richly spiced Indian curries. (p111)

Li Jiang A menu infused with the fragrant flavours of Southeast Asia. (p110)

Best Friday Brunch

Giornotte A globe-trotting foodie bonanza from oysters to Wagyu beef at the Ritz-Carlton. (p110)

Felini Garden Italian flavours, beach dune views and a wandering saxophonist to boot. (p124)

Crust Full-on international buffet of flavours at the Four Seasons. (p78)

Best Seafood

Sayad Possibly the city's finest seafood in the city's most celebrated hotel. (p62)

Catch Scandi-decor, beachfront setting and great sushi and seafood. (p63)

Zuma The pinnacle of Abu Dhabi's sushi scene. (p80)

Top Tips

Dining out can quickly empty your wallet in Abu Dhabi. Many restaurants, even some of the fine-dining venues, offer good-value business lunch set menus for half the price a meal would cost you à la carte.

Drinking & Nightlife

RICHARD CLARKE/ALAMY STOCK PHOTO ©

In a country of extreme temperatures, it's hardly surprising that the pace of life by day is slow. City-dwellers make up for it at night, however, pouring onto the Corniche at dusk and sitting out until late sipping coffee and smoking shisha. For something stronger, head to the bars, attached to either hotels or top-end restaurants.

Local Style

If you think of the picnic as an essentially daytime activity, then think again. The Emiratis, in common with people of the Gulf in general, love big parties. These generally involve going out en masse with the extended family, finding a comfortable perch, preferably outdoors, and chatting until the small hours. These ad hoc night-time picnics in Abu Dhabi's parks form the focus of city nightlife for many locals.

The Expat Way

Abu Dhabi abounds with favourite expat watering holes, and most midrange and top-end restaurants and hotels have bars serving alcohol. Nightlife for Western expats tends to revolve around these haunts, many of which offer promotions, sports on TV, ladies nights, cocktail menus and rooftop lounges. Resident DJs put in an appearance later at night and bands, generally from the Philippines, add a bit of boogie to the beat.

Best Cocktails

Hakkasan Seriously creative signature cocktails are what this place is about. (p65)

Dragon's Tooth A snug hidden den for cocktail lovers. (p80)

Asia De Cuba Sip cocktails on the terrace leading straight out to the sand. (p67)

Best Shisha

Hookah Lounge The outdoor terrace overlooking the sea is the place to be for shisha. (p55)

Escape Beer and shisha on the beach. (p66)

Yacht Gourmet Restaurant With uninterrupted views of the capital skyline, this is a shisha classic. (p66)

LINDSEY PARRY/LONELY PLANET ©

Best for Drinks with a View

Ray's Bar The skyscrapers are your neighbours at this 67th-floor bar. (p65)

Glo From October to April this rooftop overlooking Al Zahiyah's towers buzzes after dark. (p81)

Beach House Rooftop For chilled-out beach vibes you can't beat the sand and sea views here. (pictured; p98)

Chameleon Terrace Cocktails and views of the Sheikh Zayed Grand Mosque across the water. (p114)

Stratos 360-degree views of the city in this revolving lounge. (p44)

Best for Dancing

Mad on Yas Island The biggest indoor club in the UAE. (p127)

Iris DJs Thursday to Sunday for partying overlooking Yas Marina. (p128)

Empire Yas Dance on the bridge over the Formula One track. (p127)

Best Beer Drinker Haunts

Belgian Café Can't be beaten for hops, mussels and home-cut chips. (p67)

Brauhaus For all your German brew needs. (p83)

Stars 'N' Bars International craft beer selection and Yas Marina views. (p127)

McGettigan's AUH Happening Irish pub. (p127)

Top Tips

- Check out the two-for-one cocktail deals, happy hours and regular promotions that even the swankiest bars hold.
- To savour the best of Abu Dhabi's nightlife and cafe scene, don't come between mid-May and mid-September, as many venues close their outdoor terraces for the summer.

Architecture

Clustered with skyscrapers, Abu Dhabi's modern skyline is one of the most spectacular in the Middle East, representing not just outstanding design but also remarkable feats of engineering. In the capital, hotels and malls are not designed merely for function, they participate in the avant-garde aesthetic of the city.

Building on Sand

Survey the old photographs in the museum at Abu Dhabi Heritage Village, and you'll notice that less than a century ago Qasr Al Hosn was located in splendid isolation in the middle of an empty coastal plain.

The famous desert explorer Wilfred Thesiger writes of reaching a small town of 2000 inhabitants in the late 1940s after crossing the Empty Quarter. He led his faltering camels across the mud of the Khor Al Maqta as there were no bridges.

Today Qasr Al Hosn is dwarfed by downtown's high-rises, three bridges connect the mainland to Abu Dhabi Island and the city has grown to a population of around 2.5 million. This gives a measure of the pace of development from the mid-20th century to the present day.

Future Vision

Abu Dhabi's skyline is always evolving. The capital's new central business district is currently taking shape on Al Maryah Island, two more major museum projects are planned for Saadiyat Island and Masdar City is an experiment in sustainable urban living for the future.

Best Cultural Icons

Sheikh Zayed Grand Mosque The jewel in the crown of the capital. (p104)

Louvre Abu Dhabi The Louvre's interior features a rain of light. (p86)

Founder's Memorial A stunning 3D artwork anchors this memorial plaza. (p52)

Best City Towers

Burj Mohammed Bin Rashid The highest building in Abu Dhabi with a striking slanting roof. (p39)

ARCHITECT: ZAHA HADID. SOLKAFA/SHUTTERSTOCK ©

Capital Gate Currently holds the world record for the most extreme lean. (p137)

Observation Deck at 300 Whizz up to Etihad Towers' observation deck to view towers from above. (p58)

Best Contemporary Architecture

Emirates Palace Bridging the gap between modern and traditional Arab architecture. (p50)

Masdar City Showcases cutting-edge, energy-efficient architecture. (p120)

Abu Dhabi Global Market Square The focal point of the Al Maryah Island CBD development. (p74)

Sheikh Zayed Bridge Evocative of sand dunes, this bridge almost seems to move at night. (pictured above; p108)

Best Heritage Architecture

Qasr Al Hosn This fort is the oldest building in the city. (p38)

Zayed Heritage Centre One of the few examples of traditional Gulf architecture in the city. (p59)

Abu Dhabi Heritage Village Note the wind tower, an inspiration for today's eco-aware architects. (p58)

Al Maqta Fort and Watchtower Marooned amid the modernity of the Khor Al Maqta waterfront area. (p109)

Top Tips

Much of Abu Dhabi's modern architecture is neon-lit at night, making for fantastic night photography. Take an outdoor terrace seat at Yas Marina for views of the Yas Hotel's spectacular mantel straddling the Yas Marina Circuit.

Activities & Tours

Best known for the Grand Prix, Abu Dhabi has maximised on that reputation for speed, with Yas Island front and centre of theme-park fun. The water is where the best activities are though, with kayaking, stand-up paddleboarding and boating all on offer.

A Day in the Desert

The great desert explorer Wilfred Thesiger claimed that no one could live like the Bedouin in the desert and remain unchanged. To get an inkling of what he meant, a day in the sand dunes, with their rhythm and their song (some whistle when it is windy), is a wonderful way to understand both Abu Dhabi's rich Bedouin heritage and also the city's remarkable growth against the physical odds.

In Abu Dhabi the following companies offer half-day tours with dinner and overnight stays in the dunes outside Liwa Oasis.

Abu Dhabi Desert Safari (☎055 484 2001; www.abudhabi-desert-safari.com; evening desert safari per person Dhs300; ⏰7am-11.30pm) specialises in both private desert excursions (good if you have a group of at least three) and group overnight desert trips that include dinner entertainment and sandboarding opportunities.

Emirates Tours & Safari (☎02 491 2929, 24hr 050 532 6837; www.eatours.ae; city tour half/full day Dhs160/360; ⏰8am-7pm Sun-Thu) offers overnight tours in a tent with a trip to a camel farm, dinner, entertainment and sandboarding.

Best Water Activities

Noukhada Adventure Company Kayaking tours amid Mangrove National Park. (p136)

Captain Tony's Sunset cruises and boat tours. (p123)

Eywoa SUP-boarding, kite-surfing, wake-boarding and kayaking. (p124)

VLADIBUDDY/SHUTTERSTOCK ©

Dive Mahara Recreational wreck-diving trips for experienced divers. (p78)

Best City Sightseeing

Big Bus Abu Dhabi This hop-on, hop-off bus pulls in to all of Abu Dhabi's highlights. (p147)

Seawings Sightseeing on this sea-plane flight taking off from Yas Marina. (p124)

Best Dhow Cruises

Abu Dhabi Pearl Journey Own a pearl at the end of this informative dhow tour from the Eastern Mangrove Promenade. (p136)

Dhow Cruises Abu Dhabi A relaxing potter around the Breakwater in a traditional fishing vessel. (p66)

Best Adrenaline Rush

DriveYas A chance to skid your way round the famous Yas Marina Circuit. (p119)

Ferrari World Abu Dhabi Offering the fastest ride in the world, a go-kart academy and technically dazzling simulations. (p123)

Warner Bros World Abu Dhabi Spinning-top roller coasters and 5D immersive experiences. (p123)

Yas Waterworld Go in search of the lost pearl on more than 40 slides and rides. (p124)

Emirati Experiences

Organised by Abu Dhabi's Department of Culture and Tourism, the **Emirati Experiences Tours** (www.visitabudhabi.ae; tours per person Dhs50-1000) allow an insight into Emirati culture. Tours range from a food tour munching your way through the city's traditional restaurants, to a trip to a local home.

Shopping

There are regional brands if you poke around but what Abu Dhabi does well shopping-wise is international brands. The craftwork (inlaid boxes etc) you see here comes from the wider Middle East while the pashminas come from Pakistan and India. For region-specific gifts, check out the contemporary artisan stores riffing on traditional designs.

PICTAFOLIO/GETTY IMAGES ©

Best Art & Crafts

FBMI This NGO sells gorgeous handmade textiles and carpets made by Afghan women. (p129)

Julia Ibbini Studio Beautiful, original artwork fusing ancient craft with modern technology. (p44)

Gallery One Funky art prints and homewares with Middle Eastern designs. (p115)

Al Saadah Art Gallery Hand-painted ceramic tiles with both modern and traditional motifs. (p115)

Best for Foodie Shopping

Bateel Boutique Dates given the luxury treatment – smothered in chocolate or stuffed. (p115)

Fruit & Vegetable Market Dates straight from the market traders, fresh or dried. (p99)

Wafi Gourmet Middle Eastern sweets...and more dates. (p68)

Best Malls

Yas Mall It would take days to explore this massive mall properly. (p129)

Marina Mall Good international brand shopping with some more local outlets as well. (p70)

Best Local Interest

World Trade Center Souk Built on the site of the original souq, this Norman Foster–designed arcade is a delight to visit. (p44)

Souk Qaryat Al Beri A modern souq-mall with a great waterfront location. (p115)

Madinat Zayed Shopping & Gold Centre All the gold shops of Abu Dhabi collected under one roof. (p45)

Khalifa Centre A ragbag of shops selling carpets, boxes, pashminas and brass coffee pots. (p83)

Entertainment

ANDREJ ISAKOVIC/AFP/GETTY IMAGES ©

International performers stage concerts in one of two purpose-built venues. For live music, many of the hotel bars have regular cover bands on Thursday and Friday night.

Festivals & Events

For sport fans, the big sporting spectacle is the Abu Dhabi Grand Prix (p119), which also brings big name bands and singers to town for the event's evening entertainment. For classical music fans, the **Abu Dhabi Festival** (www.abudhabifestival.ae; ticket prices vary; ⌚Mar-Apr) is a month-long series of classical music and Middle Eastern musicians.

Best Stage Craft

NYUAD The Arts Center Music concerts, dance performances and film screenings. (p99)

Laughter Factory International comedy names regularly perform sets here. (p114)

Best for Live Bands

Jazz Bar & Dining Live jazz bands entertain a sage audience at this old favourite. (p68)

McGettigan's AUH This Irish bar has a lively schedule of local bands and musicians. (p127)

Pacifiko Tiki The Latin house band provides music most nights. (p127)

PJ O'Reilly's This Irish bar has three nights of live music weekly. (p44)

Heroes A no-frills old timer with a fun house band. (p44)

Top Tips

- Time Out Abu Dhabi (www.timeoutabudhabi.com) has a full listing of events.
- Tickets for concerts are available through the UAE's Ticketmaster website: www.ticketmaster.ae.

Beaches & Spas

PROCHASSON FREDERIC/SHUTTERSTOCK ©

Surrounded by water on all sides, Abu Dhabi has made the most of its beachfront location. Whether you want to sunbathe with cocktails on hand at an exclusive patch of sand, or on the well-maintained public beaches with a BYO picnic like the locals, there's a stretch of seaside for everyone.

Best Public Beaches

Saadiyat Public Beach A boardwalk leads through the protected nature sanctuary to a pristine beach. (p94)

Yas Beach A fun vibe and a great place to chill with a beer. (p123)

Corniche Beach Well-maintained and popular, with lifeguards available. (p38)

Al Bateen Beach Wide strip of sand, buzzing with families on weekends. (p136)

Best Beach Clubs

Radisson Blu Beach Club With shady palm trees, this is one of the city's most popular leisure facilities. (p60)

Nation Riviera Beach Club In a stylish cluster of buildings on the Corniche, offering a luxury day out. (p60)

Saadiyat Beach Club The infinity pool of this upmarket club is reason enough to visit. (pictured above; p94)

Nurai Island Get a day pass to hang out on the beach at this exclusive island resort. (p98)

Beach Rotana Club A low-key pleasant beach with plenty of eating and drinking options on hand. (p78)

Best Spas

ESpa The re-created Moroccan riad (traditional house) surroundings include a full traditional hammam (Turkish bath). (p110)

Anantara Spa All marble and water features for relaxation, massages and hammams. (p137)

Sense Spa A super-sophisticated, high-tech approach to indulgent bathing. (p77)

Emirates Palace Spa The ultimate in decadence with 24-carat gold applications. (p71)

For Kids

Kid-wise Abu Dhabi is best known for its theme parks and beaches, but there's more than roller coasters and sand to family travel here. Children are hugely welcome in this family-focused city, though be prepared for many of the activities to take place indoors because of the extreme heat.

PITK/SHUTTERSTOCK ©

Best for All-Weather Fun

Ferrari World Abu Dhabi Nearly everything in this theme park is indoors. (pictured above; p123)

Warner Bros World Abu Dhabi The rides and activities of this theme park are completely covered. (p123)

Bounce Abu Dhabi Epic trampoline park at Marina Mall. (p61)

Fun Works Learning is the focus of this play environment for tots. (p124)

Best Nature Encounters

Noukhada Adventure Company Kids are welcome on these kayaking tours of Mangrove National Park. (p136)

Abu Dhabi Falcon Hospital A chance to learn about falcons and meet them up close. (p140)

Best for Discovering Culture

Abu Dhabi Pearl Journey Both little ones and teens will enjoy this boat trip while learning about pearling. (p136)

Louvre Abu Dhabi There's a dedicated children's museum here. (p86)

Best Water Parks

Yas Waterworld A good haul of water slides. (p124)

Murjan Splash Park Water-guns and slides in Khalifa Park. (p110)

Best Park Life

Umm Al Emarat Park This spot has a shade house canopy walk, petting zoo and playground equipment. (p136)

Capital Gardens Mini-climbing wall and play areas in the heart of downtown. (p35)

Khalifa Park Plenty of play areas for kids make this green space popular with families. (p109)

Al Khalidiyah Garden Great playground area for little ones. (p60)

Four Perfect Days

Day 1

VEDAANT SETHIA/SHUTTERSTOCK ©

Head to **Sheikh Zayed Grand Mosque** (pictured; p104) to gawp in awe at marble magnificence. For panoramic views of its domes, move on to **Wahat Al Karama** (p108) then cross the **Khor Al Maqta** (p108) for modern-Emirati lunching at **Milas** (p111).

Stop off in **Al Mina's harbour** (p94) to see creaky fishing dhows before devoting the afternoon to exploring the globe-trotting art collection under the silver dome of the **Louvre Abu Dhabi** (p86).

Indulge in sundowners overlooking Saadiyat's sand at the **Beach House Rooftop** (p98), sample international flavours at **Sontaya** (p97) then stroll the **Corniche** (p32) to watch the lights of the looming high-rises.

Day 2

MOHAMMED SHAMAA/SHUTTERSTOCK ©

Begin with a kayaking tour of **Mangrove National Park** (p132) from the **Eastern Mangroves Promenade** (p136). Continue the nature theme with a visit to **Umm Al Emarat Park** (p136) then lunch on Middle Eastern favourites at **Café Arabia** (p137).

Head to the **UAE flagpole** (p59) for skyline snaps then visit the **heritage village** (p58), stop for shisha at **Hookah Lounge** (p55) then whizz up to **Etihad Towers observation deck** (pictured; p58) and peer down on it all from on high.

Dine at **Li Beirut** (p62) for mezze, then check out the **Founder's Memorial** (p52) after dark when it turns on its lights, before heading for cocktails at **Hakkasan** (p65).

Day 3

PHILIP LANGE/SHUTTERSTOCK ©

Start the day by getting up close to birds of prey at the **Falcon Hospital** (p140) then check out **Masdar City** (p120), a pioneering concept in environmentally sustainable living.

Grab lunch at **Nolu's Café** (p125) then head to **Yas Island**. For thrills, an afternoon at **Ferrari World** (pictured; p123) beckons, or (if you've pre-booked) get behind the wheel with **DriveYas** (p119) at the **Yas Marina Circuit** (p118). Don't fancy heart-pumping action? Sloth out on the sand of **Yas Beach** (p123).

Tuck into Italian classics at **Felini Garden** (p124) then move on to **Yas Marina** for drinks and backdrop views of Yas Hotel's spectacular lights.

Day 4

EUSAPHZAE/SHUTTERSTOCK ©

Check out downtown with its **Corniche** (p32) and old fort, **Qasr Al Hosn** (p38). Pick up souvenirs at **World Trade Center Souk** (p44) then for lunch dig into hummus and *fuul* at **Cafeteria Al Liwan** (p39).

It's chill-out time. Head to **Saadiyat Public Beach** (pictured; p94) for one of the nicest strips of sand in town. Relax, splash in the sea or hire a kayak while you enjoy this perfect swath of sand.

Beeline to nightlife hot-spot **Abu Dhabi Global Market Square** (p74) for dinner at **Dai Pai Dong** (p79) or **Coya** (p79) then stroll the **waterfront promenade** (p77) before grabbing a seat at a high-class bar for cocktails.

Need to Know

For detailed information, see Survival Guide (p142)

Currency
UAE dirham (Dhs)

Languages
Arabic, English

Visas
Free visas (30-day or 90-day depending on country of origin) available on arrival for 60 nationalities.

Money
ATMs widely available. Credit cards accepted in most hotels, restaurants and shops.

Mobile Phones
Mobile phones operate on GSM900/1800. Prepaid SIM cards with minute-and-data combo plans widely available.

Time
Gulf Standard Time (GMT/UTC plus four hours)

Tipping
Tipping is at your discretion. Service charges are added to restaurant bills. Tip hotel porters Dhs5 to Dhs10.

Daily Budget

Budget: Less than Dhs600

Budget hotel room: Dhs250–450

Cheap local eats (shawarma, vegetable curries, mezze): Dhs15–30

Mangrove kayaking tour: Dhs160

Sheikh Zayed Grand Mosque tour: free

Midrange: Dhs600–1400

Double room: Dhs500–750

Two-course dinner: Dhs150–450

One-hour dhow cruise: Dhs95

Ferrari World entry: Dhs295

Top End: More than Dhs1400

Five-star room: from Dhs1000

Fine-dining dinner: from Dhs500

Spa massage: from Dhs450

Yas Marina Circuit driving experience: from Dhs390

Useful Websites

Visit Abu Dhabi (www.visitabudhabi.ae) Excellent official visitor website for travel planning. You can also download its Visit Abu Dhabi app.

Abu Dhabi Culture (www.abudhabiculture.ae) Information on Abu Dhabi's historic sights, Emirati traditions and cultural festivals with a handy Abu Dhabi Culture app you can download.

Time Out Abu Dhabi (www.timeoutabudhabi.com) Events, information on sights and activities, plus restaurant and bar reviews.

Arriving in Abu Dhabi

Most people arrive in Abu Dhabi by plane or from Dubai. Driving from Dubai takes around 90 minutes.

✈ Abu Dhabi International Airport

The airport (pictured below) is located 30km east of the city centre on the mainland.

Taxis Dhs75 to Dhs85 to the city centre, including flagfall of Dhs25.

Bus Airport bus A1 every 40 minutes (one hour, Dhs4), terminating at City Terminal in Al Zahiyah.

Al Wahda Bus Station

Just to the south of the downtown area, next to Al Wahda Mall.

Taxis Plentiful taxis outside the entrance.

City buses Routes heading north to downtown and south to the Sheikh Zayed Grand Mosque pass through here (Dhs2 per ride).

Getting Around

Most visitors use taxis as they are frequent, metered, usually clean and relatively inexpensive. Navigation is mostly by landmark or GPS, not by street name.

Taxi

Dhs5 at flagfall plus Dhs1.82 per kilometre. Between 10pm and 6am flagfall climbs to Dhs5.50. A Dhs12 minimum fare is in effect at all times.

Car

Easy for getting between the spread-out sights, though you'll need to cope with heavy city traffic.

Bus

Abu Dhabi City Bus (www.dot.abudhabi.ae) operates 14 routes. Most fares are Dhs2.

TUPUNGATO/SHUTTERSTOCK ©

Abu Dhabi Neighbourhoods

Al Zahiyah & Al Maryah Island (p73)
Al Maryah Island is the city's new dining and nightlife hub, while Al Zahiyah hums with local life.

Louvre Abu Dhabi

Abu Dhabi Global Market Square

Corniche

Founder's Memorial

Emirates Palace

Mangrove National Park

Sheikh Zayed Grand Mosque

Marina Breakwater (p49)
Fine dining, tapering towers and chic beach clubs. Welcome to the glamorous end of town.

Downtown (p31)
The beating heart of the city, with its towers marching along the Corniche.

Al Mina & Saadiyat Island (p85)
Journey through global heritage at the Louvre, glimpse old Abu Dhabi in Al Mina, then relax on Saadiyat's beaches.

Yas Island (p117)
Where you come for fun. It's home to the Formula One Circuit, Ferrari World and Warner Bros World.

Yas Marina Circuit

Masdar City

Abu Dhabi International Airport

Abu Dhabi Falcon Hospital

Eastern Mangroves & Al Mushrif (p131)
Search out the capital's green spaces amid its mangroves and in its most beautiful park.

Sheikh Zayed Grand Mosque Area (p103)
The magnificent mosque is the inspiration hovering over this refined neighbourhood.

Explore Abu Dhabi

Worth a Trip

Abu Dhabi's Walking Tours

Etihad Towers MOHAMMED SHAMAA/SHUTTERSTOCK ©

غرفة أبوظبي
ZAYED
غرفة أبوظبي

Explore Downtown

With its mid-rises marching in rows back from the Corniche, downtown is Abu Dhabi's bustling heart. At its core is the city's oldest building, Qasr Al Hosn, and the World Trade Center, built atop the site of the capital's original souq. Join the locals, who spill onto downtown's streets at sunset, to experience Abu Dhabi's vibrant city centre.

The Short List

- ***Qasr Al Hosn (p38)*** *Delving into history at this old fort complex.*
- ***Corniche (p32)*** *Grabbing a Cyacle Bikeshare cycle and wheeling down the waterfront promenade.*
- ***Corniche Beach (p38)*** *Hanging out on this wide strip of public beach.*
- ***Cafeteria Al Liwan (p39)*** *Sampling Syrian-style Middle Eastern dishes for wallet-friendly feasting.*
- ***Bait El Khetyar (p40)*** *Snaffling a pavement table and filling up on falafel and hummus.*

Getting There & Around

Most visitors use metered taxis to get around downtown.

Various buses service downtown but they're often crowded when boarding here. The Big Bus tour bus stops on the Corniche by the Sheraton, the World Trade Center, Al Hosn Fort and beside Markaziyah Gardens.

Cyacle offers bike shares on the Corniche.

Downtown Map on p39

Downtown Abu Dhabi MOHAMAD KADDOURA/GETTY IMAGES ©

Top Sight

Corniche

The Corniche, with its white-sand beaches and spectacular views of high-rise towers, stretches the entire length of the northwest shore of the city. This is where locals come for fresh air, exercise, cycling and family time either on the waterfront promenade or, across the road, in one of the landscaped gardens. Join in with Abu Dhabi at play.

MAP P36, E2

Going the Distance

From end to end the Corniche measures 8km, and every inch of this beautifully landscaped promenade can be walked, cycled or skated. The Founder's Memorial (a tribute to Sheikh Zayed, founding father of the UAE) is located at the western end, and along the route scented tree jasmine, orange-flowering cordias, and pastel-blossomed tabubias grace the flower-beds, offering shaded respite from the heat. In saying that, don't even think of trying to do a Corniche walk in daylight hours from May to September. Do as the locals do and wait for sunset.

Between Skylines

Walk the Corniche and you get the odd sense that you are stepping along the crease between man-made verticals and nature's horizontals. Offering the best vantage point to review the dramatic inland skyline, the Corniche is punctuated with spectacular buildings such as the World Trade Center, Nation Towers and Etihad Towers. They loom over the pavements, casting a welcome shadow on the flat-lining sea beyond.

Fun for the Family

While the sea draws the attention of most visitors, the inland side of the Corniche is worth a visit too. Dotted with parks, play areas and shisha cafes, it comes alive at night with local families seeking the sea breeze in the sweltering summer (May to September) or clustered around mobile heaters in winter (December to February). Of all these tree-lined spaces, Lake Park (p38) is one of the most popular spots due to its fountains, lake and manicured gardens.

★ Top Tips

- Bicycles can be hired on the Corniche from various bike-share Cyacle stations (www.bikeshare.ae).
- As well as the free part of the public beach, there are two separate, enclosed sections with a nominal fee where you can also hire a sun bed and umbrella.
- Access the waterfront promenade from one of the pedestrian underpasses that connect with the parks on the other side of Corniche Rd.
- Always carry water for a long stroll on the Corniche. There are long stretches with no cafes.

Take a Break

On the beach, head to Nova Beach Café (p41) for snacks, cold drinks and coffee.

In Urban Park, take a seat pond-side at Colombiano Coffee House (p35).

Walking Tour

Downtown's Heart

Locals say, 'Walk Electra and Hamdan and you've walked the city'. Trace these parallel, frenetic east–west roads, and you gain an instant sense of the bustling downtown. For something greener and more offbeat though, the following route passes by some of the parks where families come to play and the little mosques are dwarfed by the dazzling high-rises.

Walk Facts

Start Al Markaziyah Gardens

End Capital Gardens

Length 3.5km; one hour

❶ Park & Walk

Spread over three distinct areas – Al Nahyan Park, Family Park and Urban Park – **Al Markaziyah Gardens** (Corniche Rd (West); 24hr) forms a broad band of recreational lawns parallel to the Corniche. These are the lungs of the city and, with their fountains and shaded seating, offer a great place to start a healthy constitutional.

❷ Coffee Break

It may only be a couple of blocks, but reaching Urban Park from Al Nahyan Park will seem like an accomplishment for much of the year, when heat competes with humidity to be the quintessential Gulf experience. Thankfully, sociable **Colombiano Coffee House** (02 633 7765; www.cchuae.com; Corniche Rd (West), Urban Park; 9am-2am;) has comfortable waterside armchairs and thirst-quenching cold juices.

❸ Monuments of Downtown

At **Al Itihad Square** (Sheikh Rashid Bin Saeed Al Maktoum St), pause to take in the juxtaposition of the little gold-toned stone-brick mosque with its octagonal minaret, backed by the blue-hued towers of the central business district. This mosque is one of the older ones in this district. At sunset when its minaret is green-lit against the high-rises, it makes for dramatic photos.

❹ Pastry Stop

Local families love coming to **La Brioche Café** (02 627 1932; www.labriocheuae.com; Khalifa Bin Zayed the First St; breakfast Dhs25-59, mains Dhs37-89; 6am-midnight;) for a coffee and baked goods treat. Check out its counter of croissants and pain au chocolat, and you'll probably be tempted yourself.

❺ Hidden Plaza

Scoot off Khalifa St to find a lovely plaza bookended by mosques, including pretty **Abdullah Hamaid Al Rumaithi Mosque** (off Khalifa St). Note how it sits angled (facing the direction of Mecca) against the looming high-rises that dwarf the minarets. Sit in the plaza at sunset to watch crowds pile into the mosques as the last light shimmers on the surrounding towers.

❻ City at Play

Families beeline to the giant coffeepot front gate of **Capital Gardens** (Sultan Bin Zayed the First St; adult/child Dhs1/free; 8am-10pm Sun-Wed, to 11pm Thu-Sat;) when the worst of the day's heat is done to let the kids run free, cycle and play on the swings. Local teens use the sports court here for casual football and basketball games while families picnic on the park benches by the erupting fountain.

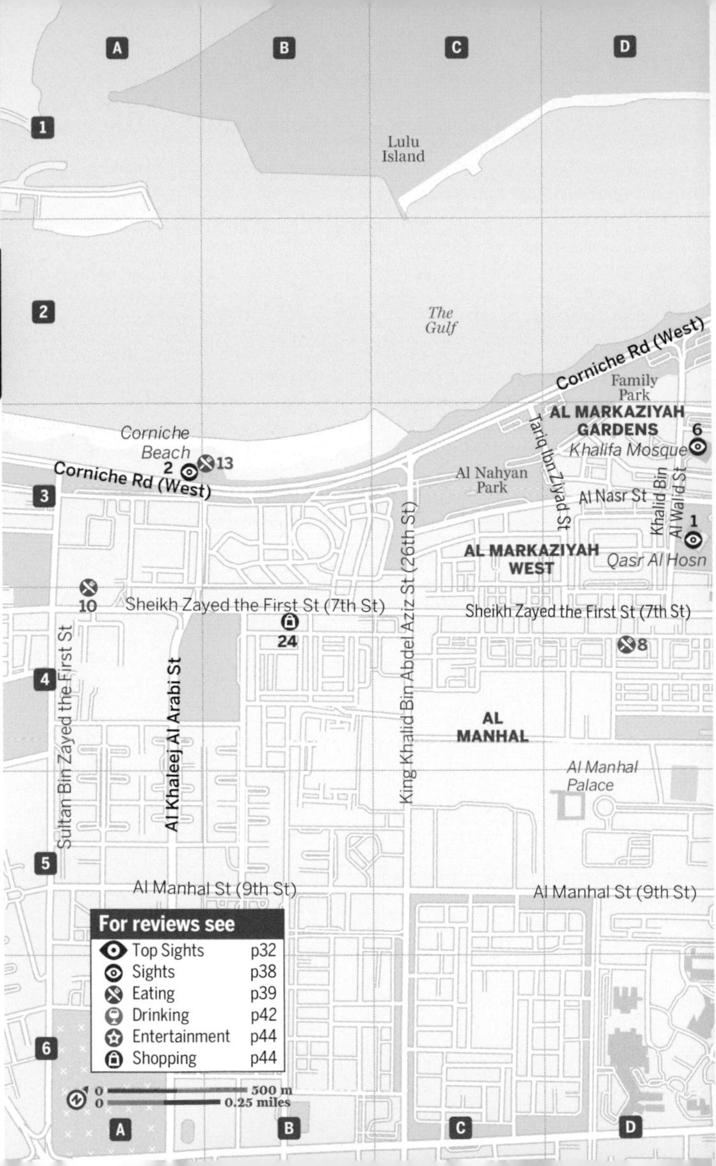

A B C D
1
2
3
4
5
6

Lulu Island
The Gulf
Corniche Rd (West)
Family Park
AL MARKAZIYAH GARDENS
Khalifa Mosque
6
Corniche Beach
2
13
Tariq Ibn Ziyad St
Al Nahyan Park
Al Nasr St
Khalid Bin Al Walid St
1
AL MARKAZIYAH WEST
Qasr Al Hosn
10
Sheikh Zayed the First St (7th St)
24
8
Sultan Bin Zayed the First St
Al Khaleej Al Arabi St
King Khalid Bin Abdel Aziz St (26th St)
AL MANHAL
Al Manhal Palace
Al Manhal St (9th St)

For reviews see

Top Sights	p32
Sights	p38
Eating	p39
Drinking	p42
Entertainment	p44
Shopping	p44

0 500 m
0 0.25 miles

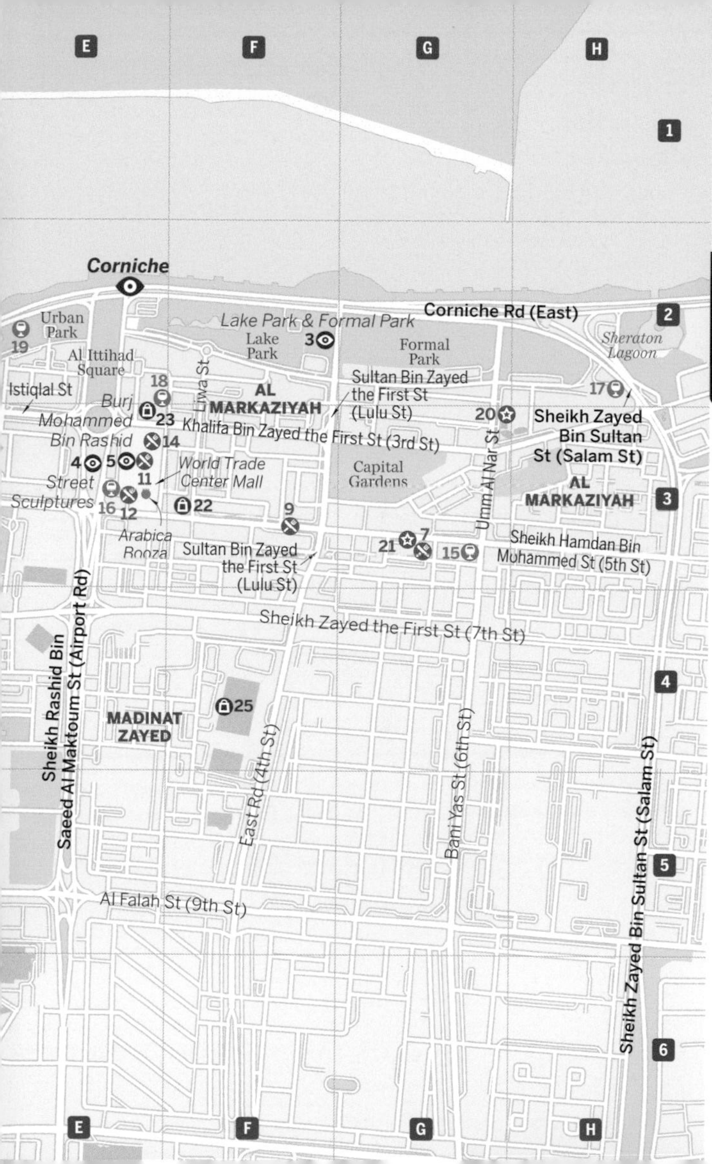

E F G H

1 2 3 4 5 6

Corniche

Corniche Rd (East)

Urban Park

19

Lake Park & Formal Park

Lake Park

3

Formal Park

Sheraton Lagoon

Al Ittihad Square

Istiqlal St

18

Liwa St

AL MARKAZIYAH

Sultan Bin Zayed the First St (Lulu St)

17

Burj Mohammed Bin Rashid

23

Khalifa Bin Zayed the First St (3rd St)

20

Sheikh Zayed Bin Sultan St (Salam St)

14

Umm Al Nar St

4 5

World Trade Center Mall

Capital Gardens

11

AL MARKAZIYAH

Street Sculptures

16 12

22

9

Arabica Booza

Sultan Bin Zayed the First St (Lulu St)

21 7

15

Sheikh Hamdan Bin Mohammed St (5th St)

Sheikh Zayed the First St (7th St)

Sheikh Rashid Bin Saeed Al Maktoum St (Airport Rd)

MADINAT ZAYED

25

East Rd (4th St)

Bani Yas St (6th St)

Sheikh Zayed Bin Sultan St (Salam St)

Al Falah St (9th St)

E F G H

Sights

Qasr Al Hosn FORT

1 MAP P36, D3

Featured on the back of the Dhs1000 note, this fort started life in 1760 as a watchtower that safeguarded a precious freshwater well. After an expansion, it became the ancestral home of the ruling Al Nahyan family in 1793 and remained a royal residence until 1966 (its watchtower is Abu Dhabi's oldest surviving structure). An extensive years-long restoration ground to the finish line in late 2018 and it was reopened as a cultural hub with historic exhibits and gallery space. (White Fort; 02 697 6472; www.alhosn.ae; Sheikh Zayed the First St; admission free; 9am-8pm)

Ice Cream Stop

You might hear the **Arabica Booza kiosk** (Map p36, E3; 055 155 6295; ground fl, World Trade Center Mall; small cup from Dhs15; 10am-10pm), serving up *booza* (Middle Eastern ice cream), before you see it. Staff wield a giant wooden pestle, rhythmically beating like a drum not only to attract attention but also to soften the ice cream. The original cream flavour is the hero, topped with pistachios as is traditional.

Corniche Beach BEACH

2 MAP P36, A3

There are several gates to this spotlessly maintained, blue-flagged public beach. The turquoise sea, view of Lulu Island, palm trees and gardens make it an unexpected pleasure in the heart of a capital city. A lifeguard is on duty until sunset. (Corniche Rd (West); family beaches adult/child Dhs10/5; 8am-8pm)

Lake Park & Formal Park PARK

3 MAP P36, F2

These two shady parks straddling 4th St and spreading along the Corniche fill up with families, joggers and picnickers in the early evening. The centrepiece of Lake Park is the 15m-high fountain; there is also a popular cafe beside the lake (though it was closed and awaiting new owners when we were last in town). In late 2018 the playground area here was being rejuvenated. Formal Park has a maze, barbecue pits and an exercise track. (Corniche Rd (East); admission free; 24hr)

Street Sculptures MONUMENT

4 MAP P36, E3

There was a time when no self-respecting Gulf city would be seen without a giant concrete coffeepot. Those days have gone, for better or for worse, but a little reminder of the pioneering days of oil riches and the city development they brought can be seen in the traffic island between the World Trade Center and Etisalat buildings. (2nd & Khalifa Sts)

Burj Mohammed Bin Rashid
NOTABLE BUILDING

5 MAP P36, E3

Stare up – access is limited to residents – at this 92-floor, 382m landmark tower which forms part of the World Trade Center and is Abu Dhabi's tallest building. The tower is the taller of two matching towers with distinctive sloping, elliptical roofs that look remarkable when lit at night. (Khalifa Bin Zayed the First St)

Khalifa Mosque
MOSQUE

6 MAP P36, D3

In common with all mosques in the city, this beautiful mosque stands in nonalignment with the grid system, honouring the direction of Mecca instead. It is closed to non-Muslims. (Khalid Bin Al Walid St)

Eating

Cafeteria Al Liwan
SYRIAN $

7 MAP P36, G3

This budget canteen will exceed your expectations every chance it gets. This is Middle Eastern flavours Syrian-style, with some of Abu Dhabi's best hummus and *fuul* (mashed fava beans), falafel fried to crispy perfection and *kawaj* (tomato and mincemeat casserole) that would make a Damascene mamma proud. It's all served in a slightly beaten but welcoming environment with graffitied walls. (02 622 1250; www.facebook.com/liwanabudhabi; off Sheikh Hamdan Bin Mohammed St; mezze Dhs12-19, mains Dhs20-40; 8.30am-11.30pm Sun-Thu, noon-1am Fri;)

Qasr Al Hosn (p38)

Zahrat Lebnan

LEBANESE $

8 MAP P36, D4

Amid a cluster of Middle Eastern snack and grill outlets, a short walk from the Qasr Al Hosn, the Lebanese Flower is a local legend, attracting a multinational clientele of city residents who come here for mezze feasts of stuffed vine leaves, falafel, hummus, and *fatayer* (stuffed mini-pastries), generously portioned kebab and shawarma plates, and cheap sandwiches. You can't go wrong. (Lebanese Flower; 02 667 5924; near Zayed the First St, Al Manhal; mezze & sandwiches Dhs8-36, mains Dhs18-55; 8am-3am;)

Bait El Khetyar

MIDDLE EASTERN $

9 MAP P36, F3

This place buzzes after dark when families pack the street-side tables, eating big shawarma plates with salad and hummus, while takeaway customers wait inside as their falafel and shawarma sandwiches are getting made. It's busy, cheap and always solidly good. Its other **branch** (02 633 3200; Fatima Bint Mubarak St) is just as popular. (Sheikh Hamdan Bin Mohammed St; sandwiches & shawarma Dhs6-27, mains Dhs24-37; 8am-1am;)

1762

CAFE $

10 MAP P36, A4

Industrial chic meets comfy Victoriana at this welcoming deli-cafe where exposed piping, bare bulb lighting, chandeliers and chalkboards with ornate frames rub up against each other. The menu is all about breakfasts, salads, sandwiches and wraps with cool combos like the *zaatar* chicken and halloumi toastie. The coffee is excellent. It's in the residential complex square behind the Oryx Hotel. (www.1762.ae; ground fl, Al Ain Tower; mains Dhs32-40; 8am-6pm Sun-Thu, 9am-10pm Fri & Sat;)

Tamba

INDIAN $$

11 MAP P36, E3

Despite the mall location this is a classy, dim-lit joint that takes the flavours of the subcontinent and adds contemporary tweaks. Get stuck into masala-rubbed Wagyu beef or Mangalorean-style chicken. If vegetarian is more your thing, order up small plates of *paneer makhani* (paneer in a creamy tomato and cashew sauce) and sweet and sour pumpkin. (02 672 8888; www.tambarestaurant.com; 6th fl, The Hub, World Trade Center Mall; mains Dhs42-232; noon-1am Sun-Thu, to 2am Fri & Sat; P)

Fifth Street Cafe

CAFE $$

12 MAP P36, E3

It's not surprising this cafe is a popular pit-stop for office workers at lunch: it's one of Hamdan Street's best bets for good coffee and has a menu selection with something for everyone. Breakfasts here run from chia pudding to eggs Benedict Middle Eastern–style, while for lunch or dinner the menu skates from sandwiches

Shisha Smoking

In Abu Dhabi two sensations mark the humid air of an Arabian evening: the wreaths of apple-scented smoke that spiral above the coffee houses and the low gurgle of water in the base of a water pipe. Shisha cafes are spread across the sea rim from the Corniche's inland parks to the terraces of Breakwater and offer a relaxing, nonalcoholic cafe experience.

Shisha smoking, also known as hookah or hubble-bubble, originated hundreds of years ago in Persia and India. Across the region shisha cafes are often a male affair. In Abu Dhabi, however, these cafes attract mixed company and solo women will feel comfortable.

There is a popular misconception that because the smoke passes through water it is somehow filtered of toxins, but this is not the case. In fact, doctors argue that shisha is worse for your health than cigarettes, not least because a typical shisha session lasts for an hour and involves 200 puffs of nicotine, compared with only 20 for a regular cigarette.

to corn-fed chicken with parmesan mash. (☎02 698 2222; Sheikh Hamdan bin Mohammed St, Courtyard by Marriott World Trade Center; mains Dhs35-105; 🕐7am-11pm; 📶)

Cho Gao — ASIAN $$

This upbeat joint at the Crowne Plaza Abu Dhabi (see 21 Map P36, G3), is a favourite for its tasty fare, which hopscotches from Japan to Singapore and China to Thailand. Whether you're in the mood for a mango salad, Vietnamese-style noodles or Peking duck, it's got you covered. It's all fresh and flavourful, though typically spicy dishes such as laksa have, disappointingly, been seriously toned down. (☎02 616 6149; www.facebook.com/chogaoasianexperience; Sheikh Hamdan Bin Mohammed St, ground fl, Crowne Plaza Abu Dhabi; mains Dhs50-130; 🕐noon-1am; 📶🍸)

Nova Beach Café — CAFE $$

13 MAP P36, B3

A devoted local following fills this cafe, one of the few public places where you can have a coffee or meal overlooking the sea. If you're walking or cycling the Corniche, or looking for a bite between swims, this is a sociable venue where you can catch the sea breeze. The menu covers all the bases from noodles and curry to sandwiches. (☎02 658 1870; www.facebook.com/novabeachcafe; Corniche Beach, Corniche Rd (West); mains Dhs37-93; 🕐9am-11pm; 📶)

Crossing Downtown's Roads

To avoid waiting for ages at traffic light intersections to cross the road, look for the pedestrian underpasses positioned – usually mid-block – along big main roads like Sheikh Hamdan Bin Mohammed St. There are also underpasses (often with groovy tile art) between the parks and the waterfront promenade all along the Corniche.

Bu! LATIN AMERICAN $$$

14 MAP P36, E3

Book ahead for a table at this trendy pan-Latin restaurant-bar, inside the World Trade Center Mall. It has excellent ceviche, fish and lobster tacos and other festive Latin staples (Brazilian fish stews, Peruvian fried rices, Argentine beef cuts); the salsa and merengue music ensure the mood is merry. (02 666 8066; www.butrinity.com; 4th fl, The Hub, World Trade Center Mall; mains Dhs95-285; 5pm-1am Sat-Wed, to 3am Thu, 12.30-4.30pm & 5pm-1am Fri;)

Market Kitchen INTERNATIONAL $$$

Cosy dining, complete with a tree sprouting in the middle of the restaurant, and a mezzanine-level bar area. Concentrating on bistro-style cooking, dishes like parmesan-crusted chicken, roasted beetroot salad sprinkled with crystallised ginger, and soy-glazed beef short ribs with apple and jalapeno purée head up a menu filled with creative flair. Market Kitchen, located in the Royal Meridien (see 20 Map P36, G3), is one cool, contemporary customer. (www.marketkitchenabudhabi.com; Khalifa Bin Zayed the First St, Le Royal Méridien; mains Dhs76-195; noon-4pm & 7-11pm Sat-Wed, to midnight Thu & Fri;)

Drinking

Cafe 302 CAFE

15 MAP P36, G3

We really like this cafe, fronted by a small streetfront terrace, for its cracking coffee, cooling milkshakes and good tea selection. The taupe and white brick interior is a soothing escape from the Hamdan St traffic bustle. Avoid breakfast time (or sit outside) as it's used as the breakfast space for Al Maha Arjaan hotel's guests and is too busy. (02 610 6666; Sheikh Hamdan bin Mohammed St, Al Maha Arjaan Rotana Hotel; 6am-10pm;)

Up & Below ROOFTOP BAR

16 MAP P36, E3

Have a beer (Dhs34 to Dhs40) or wine (glass from Dhs35) with high-rises as your neighbours at this bar on the roof of the World Trade Center; entry is through the Marriott. There's an easygoing, relaxed vibe with a background of chill-out music and some quirky cocktails (Dhs50 to Dhs70) to boot. (Sheikh Hamdan Bin Mohammed

St, Courtyard by Marriott World Trade Center; 11am-2am;)

Jazz & Fizz Bar

BAR

17 MAP P36, H2

There's a pianist playing tunes on weeknights for a relaxed ambience: kick back on one of the sofas and stare out at cityscape views from this bar on the 36th floor. You'll nearly always find a drinks promotion of some kind on here, and live bands usually play on Thursday and Friday. (02 813 7777; Corniche (East), Sofitel Abu Dhabi; 5pm-3pm;)

Raw Place

JUICE BAR

18 MAP P36, E2

It's pricey, but this organic, cold-pressed-juice chain churns out some seriously tasty bevvies fashioned from all manner of fresh fruits, vegetables and herbs (as well as nut milks, ginger shots and matcha). Once temperatures begin soaring, you won't care how much they cost. (www.therawplace.com; World Trade Center Souk; 7am-11pm Sun-Thu, from 8am Fri)

Level Lounge

BAR

This relaxing poolside rooftop lounge at the Crowne Plaza Abu Dhabi (see **21** Map P36, G3) reopened after a full makeover in 2018. New glass partitions and ceilings offer a piece of tower-top calm and cool even in the summer in the middle of the hectic city. It's a good local haunt for shisha and a chat with chill-out music. (02 616 6101; www.crowneplaza.com; Sheikh Hamdan

World Trade Center Mall

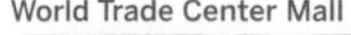

Bin Mohammed St, Crowne Plaza Abu Dhabi; 7pm-2am;)

Stratos LOUNGE

Quaff wine (glass from Dhs40) or a classic whisky sour (cocktails Dhs50 to Dhs65) and watch the city slowly pass by at this revolving lounge in the Royal Meridien (see 20 Map P36, G3). It's a plush set-up with booths of high-backed chairs, all with window views. (800 101 101; www.stratosabudhabi.com; Khalifa Bin Zayed the First St, Le Royal Méridien Abu Dhabi; 5pm-late Sun-Fri;)

Tiara Resto Café CAFE

19 MAP P36, E2

This small cafe in Urban Park has an outside terrace looking onto the park's fountains It's a decent spot for a late-night coffee and chat with friends while puffing on a shisha (Dhs55) – try the double apple or rose flavours. (Corniche Rd (West), Urban Park, Al Markaziyah Gardens; 10am-1am;)

Entertainment

PJ O'Reilly's LIVE MUSIC

20 MAP P36, G3

This popular Irish pub, with a poolside outdoor area, is a good spot for those seeking out live music, with bands playing every Wednesday, Thursday and Friday night. Wednesday is also ladies night, with complimentary house beverages. (www.pjspubabudhabi.com; Khalifa Bin Zayed the First St, Le Royal Méridien; noon-2am Sat-Wed, to 3am Thu & Fri;)

Heroes LIVE MUSIC

21 MAP P36, G3

This old-timer doesn't need chi-chi designer interiors or a fancy-pants cocktail list put together by a world-famous mixologist to pull punters in. Heroes has a rocking house band that gets the party started most nights of the week. And it can get packed in here. A fun, down-to-earth, no-posing kind of place. (02 418 2474; Sheikh Hamdan bin Mohammed St, Crowne Plaza Abu Dhabi; noon-4am;)

Shopping

Julia Ibbini Studio ART

22 MAP P36, F3

Make an appointment in advance through the website to view Julia Ibbini's complex, multi-layered artworks in her studio. Her pieces, which riff on the geometric patterns of Middle Eastern artistry, are created using a mix of digital design and traditional craftsmanship. They're a completely unique souvenir of your UAE trip. (055 609 3775; www.ibbini.com; Du Bldg, Sheikh Hamdan Bin Mohammed St; by appointment)

World Trade Center Souk MALL

23 MAP P36, E3

British architect Norman Foster's immensely pleasant reinterpretation of the traditional souq is a

Shopping for Gold

Although the style of gold jewellery displayed in the gold souq of Madinat Zayed Shopping & Gold Centre isn't to everyone's taste (think heavily ornamental yellow gold), for those who are eager to shop rather than simply browse, handcrafted pieces can be bought for a fraction of what it would cost back home.

This is because gold (here usually of around 23 carat) is bought by weight while the cost of the fine handicraft of each piece of jewellery is usually free. So when you buy bangles, necklaces and other items by weight, no extra cost is added for the complexity of design or quality of workmanship. Check the price of gold online before you go to get a rough idea of the expected price.

Note that in Islamic tradition, it is *haram* (forbidden) for men to wear gold – they usually wear silver.

stylish composition of warm lattice woodwork, stained glass, walkways and balconies. On the site of the old central market, it connects with the modern World Trade Center Mall (p42). (www.wtcad.ae; Khalifa Bin Zayed the First St; 10am-10pm Sat-Wed, to 11pm Thu & Fri;)

Eclectic ANTIQUES

24 MAP P36, B4

A delightful browsing experience with old furniture and textiles hobnobbing with new paintings, ceramics and sculpture by local Gulf artists. It's a royal pain to find, but it's on the mezzanine level (level 0 in the lift) of the Patchi shop building. (02 666 5158; www.facebook.com/eclectic.antiques.and.furniture; cnr Zayed the First St & Sha'm St; 10.30am-2pm & 5-9pm Sat-Wed, 11-7pm Thu)

Madinat Zayed Shopping & Gold Centre MARKET

25 MAP P36, F4

For first-time visitors to a gold souq, the window displays of bridal necklaces, earrings and belts, the trays of precious stones and the tiers of gold bangles in this old-fashioned shopping centre are an attraction in their own right. It's also known for being a place to shop for affordable pearls set in gold necklaces and rings. (www.madinatzayed-mall.com; 4th St; 9am-10.30pm Sun-Thu, 4-10.30pm Fri)

Walking Tour

Walking the Corniche

Stroll along the sea, enjoying the landscaped gardens of the Corniche, singing birds and scented trees, and soon the busy metropolis will seem a world away. That said, there isn't a better way to admire the modern architecture of downtown Abu Dhabi. Attempt this route in the early morning or evening in summer to avoid the excessive heat.

Walking Facts

Start Abu Dhabi Flag; Marina Mall bus stop

Finish Heritage Park; Sheraton bus stop

Length 10.5km; four hours

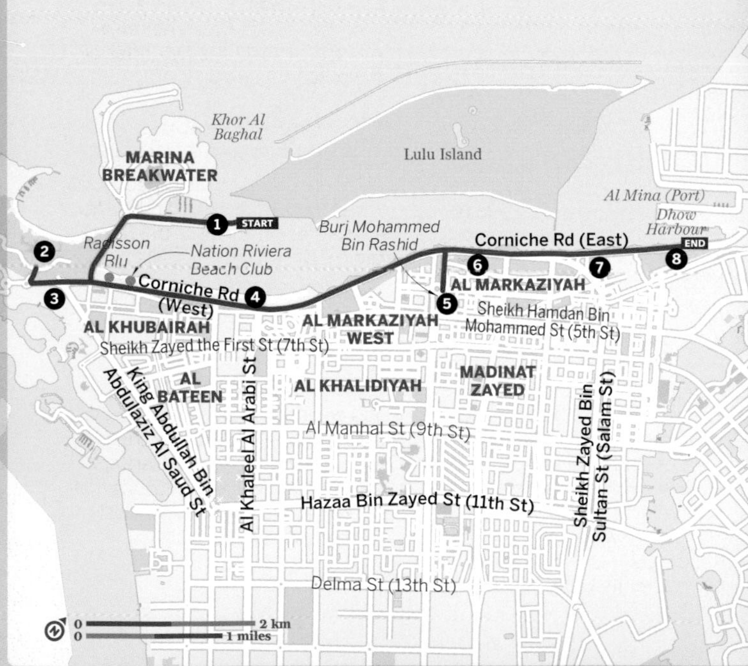

❶ Abu Dhabi Heritage Village

From the giant flag, the symbol of unity in this capital city, it's a brief stroll to the Abu Dhabi Heritage Village (p58). Here you can enjoy a glimpse of Emirati life before oil revenues transformed the country forever.

❷ Breakwater

Stroll along the breakwater. The view beyond is dominated by the opulent Emirates Palace (p50) – hotel, spa, cultural centre and general city icon.

❸ Founder's Memorial

Joining the Corniche, you come to the Founder's Memorial (p52), commemorating Sheikh Zayed, father of the nation. His 'benign dictatorship' single-handedly developed Abu Dhabi and the country as a whole. The memorial plaza is centred around a massive 3D artwork which reveals an abstract portrait of Sheikh Zayed when approached from the right.

❹ Corniche Beach

Walking along the Corniche (or you can cycle from here), you'll see similar expressions of confidence, such as Nation Towers, home to the St Regis. The Hiltonia and the Nation Riviera Beach Clubs offer luxurious swimming; the Corniche Beach (p38) is free and blue-flagged for its cleanliness.

❺ World Trade Center

Take a break at the Nova Beach Café and pause next at Rashid Bin Saeed Al Maktoum St. The inland procession of fine buildings includes the Burj Mohammed Bin Rashid (p39), the city's tallest tower and home to the World Trade Centre Mall, and the Etisalat building with its 'golf ball' crown.

❻ Al Markaziyah Gardens (East)

This stretch is beautifully landscaped and parallels attractive gardens, like Lake Park (p38), inland. Pedestrian underpasses (complete with awesome retro tile-art) connect the two sides of the road.

❼ Sheraton Lagoon

In a city where the shoreline has been dredged and reshaped at will, it's endearing to see that the *khor* (desert lagoon) beside the Sheraton (p78) has not been filled in. In fact, the Corniche passes over it leaving this venerable hotel with its treasured beach.

❽ Dhow Harbour

You could end here (there's a cycle station and a bus stop by the Sheraton) or continue on to Heritage Park (p77) and a romantic view of the dhows floating two-abreast in the harbour opposite.

Explore Marina Breakwater

Whether you're snapping pics on the beach beside the heritage village or have zoomed up 300m in the elevator to Etihad Towers' observation deck, this neighbourhood is where you come for epic city views. A more subtle attraction is the Founder's Memorial: visit after dark when the lit-up 3D monument reveals its clever artistry, backdropped by more neon-stripped high-rise vistas.

The Short List

- ***Founder's Memorial (p52)*** *Marvelling at the clever 3D portrait hidden within this tribute to the UAE's founding father.*
- ***Emirates Palace (p50)*** *Gawping at glitzy interiors before snapping iconic skyscraper shots from the garden's grand staircase entry.*
- ***Observation Deck at 300 (p58)*** *Peering down at skyscrapers and out to the arid plains beyond from the dizzying heights of Etihad Tower 2's 74th floor.*
- ***Ray's Bar (p65)*** *Sipping sunset cocktails with one of the best high-rise vistas in town.*
- ***Li Beirut (p62)*** *Diving into the fresh flavours of Levantine dining with a mezze feast fit for a pasha.*

Getting There & Around

Bus 34 is one of several routes that connects Breakwater with the Corniche at Al Khalidiyah. Bus 9 connects Breakwater with Al Bateen. The Big Bus tour bus connects the Corniche Beach, Heritage Village, Marina Mall and Etihad Towers.

Marina Breakwater Map on p56

Etihad Towers MONTICELLO/SHUTTERSTOCK ©

Top Sight

Emirates Palace

Wallet not padded enough to sleep sweetly in the lap of luxury with butler service at hand? The public areas of this Dhs11 billion crashpad are open for all. This is the region's big-name hotel, its architecture an audacious pastiche of the grand, glamorous hotels of old. Stand amid the soaring domed foyer and bathe in Gulf glitz.

MAP P56, B3

02 690 9000

www.emiratespalace.com

Corniche Rd (West)

admission free

Architectural Style

At Emirates Palace, there's far more of the 'Palace' than the 'Emirates'. The enormous multi-winged, cupola-clad, red-stone building could be mistaken for a flight of 19th-century Orientalist fancy from Western Europe rather than anything distinctively Emirati. That's not a criticism: in the Gulf you rarely encounter such an ambitious horizontal building project these days.

Statistics

The Dhs11 billion (US$3.5 billion) construction price tag gives Emirates Palace a place in the top five most expensive hotels ever built. Nearly 115 domes grace the roof line, with the grand dome of the foyer soaring to 60m high. At the core of the hotel, the foyer is opulently decorated with marble, silver and gold glass mosaic tiles and 22-carat gold-leaf gilding (Emirates Palace holds the record for the largest expanse of gilding work covering one building).

Good as Gold

The Emirates Palace has a thing about gold. Not only is there a lobby ATM that dispenses solid gold bars (yes, really!), the precious metal also turns up in unexpected places. The signature 24-carat cappuccino is sprinkled with it, the molten chocolate cake is a lava of gold, the camel burgers are packed in gold-dusted buns, and you can even get yourself covered in the stuff. It's the kind of place you imagine a villain from a classic James Bond film would choose to go on holiday to.

A Cultural Icon

Hosting opera and renowned orchestras during the Abu Dhabi Classics concert season, and showing screenings during the Abu Dhabi Film Festival, the Emirates Palace plays a regular part in the cultural expansion of the capital.

★ Top Tips

- You don't have to be a millionaire to stay at the Emirates Palace. Look for bargain packages in summer.
- Reservations are recommended for all of the Emirates Palace's restaurants.
- Coming here for gold-sprinkled coffee at Le Café? If you're visiting in the cooler months, grab a table at its outdoor cafe (beside the hotel entrance fountains) rather than inside the lobby, for great skyscraper views.

Take a Break

Not surprisingly, tempting breaks abound in the Emirates Palace. High tea in Le Café (p64) is a city institution, while coffee options include a camelccino, made with camel's milk.

For fine-dining spins on local cuisine, Mezlai (p62) offers the most refined Emirati dishes in town.

Top Sight

Founder's Memorial

The Founder's Memorial is one of the cleverest pieces of public art in the Gulf region. The central monument inside this manicured plaza is a massive prism-shaped pavilion strung with cables, with geometric shapes suspended upon their length. Seen from the correct angle, they create a 3D image of Sheikh Zayed: a very modern memorial for the founding father of the UAE.

MAP P56, C4

02 222 2235

www.thefoundersmemorial.ae

cnr Corniche Rd & Breakwater Rd

admission free

9am-10pm

Sheikh Zayed

Sheikh Zayed Bin Sultan Al Nahyan, both ruler of the emirate of Abu Dhabi and the founder, as well as first president, of the UAE, remains venerated today across the country. This contemporary memorial is a fittingly modern tribute for a man who moved the Trucial States into modern statehood and created present-day Abu Dhabi from, basically, scratch. You can watch a multimedia presentation on Sheikh Zayed at the memorial's visitors centre.

The Constellation

This avant-garde artwork (pictured), created by American artist Ralph Helmick, is the centrepiece of the memorial plaza. Nearly 1330 geometric shapes dangle on 1110 cables strung from top to bottom of the monumental stone pavilion, creating an abstract portrait of Sheikh Zayed when seen from the right angle. The geometric shapes used to create the image are all platonic solids (the five regular, convex polyhedron shapes) whose perfect mathematics have fascinated humans since ancient Greece. As well as the shapes forming a 3D image, the artist's vision was that they also individually represent the night sky's stars, collectively becoming a celestial display. After sunset, 1203 up-lights and 753 down-lights illuminate the artwork to create the effect.

Memorial Plaza

The Constellation sits in the middle of a landscaped plaza, planted with native plants such as ghaf and sidr trees, sweet acacia and umbrella thorn. A water channel feature, inspired by the UAE's traditional *falaj* (irrigation channel) system, runs from the main entrance to the pavilion. The plaza is rimmed by an elevated walkway enabling visitors to view the artwork from a more on-level perspective.

★ Top Tips

- You want to see this after dark, when the geometric shapes are lit up, making the 3D portrait more defined. It also makes for a fantastically dramatic photograph.
- The angle where the portrait is revealed is from the Corniche Rd–facing side.
- Stroll the length of the elevated walkway around to the back for great views of both the Emirates Palace and Etihad Towers; it's particularly great for night-time shots when these two Abu Dhabi icons have a rainbow neon-off.

Take a Break

Zoom up the lift to Ray's Bar (p65) for more night vista viewing, this time from above.

For waterfront views, plus shisha, head to Hookah Lounge (p55).

Walking Tour

A Photographer's Seaboard Journey

You can't claim to have visited Abu Dhabi if you haven't engaged with the sea. The sea defines life here and is a reminder of the city's seafaring heritage. This seaboard route gives you a fish-eyed view of the neighbourhood. Start late in the afternoon for changing shoreline views as the sun sets and the high-rises turn their neon on.

Walk Facts

Start UAE Flagpole

End Asia De Cuba

Length 3 km; 45 minutes

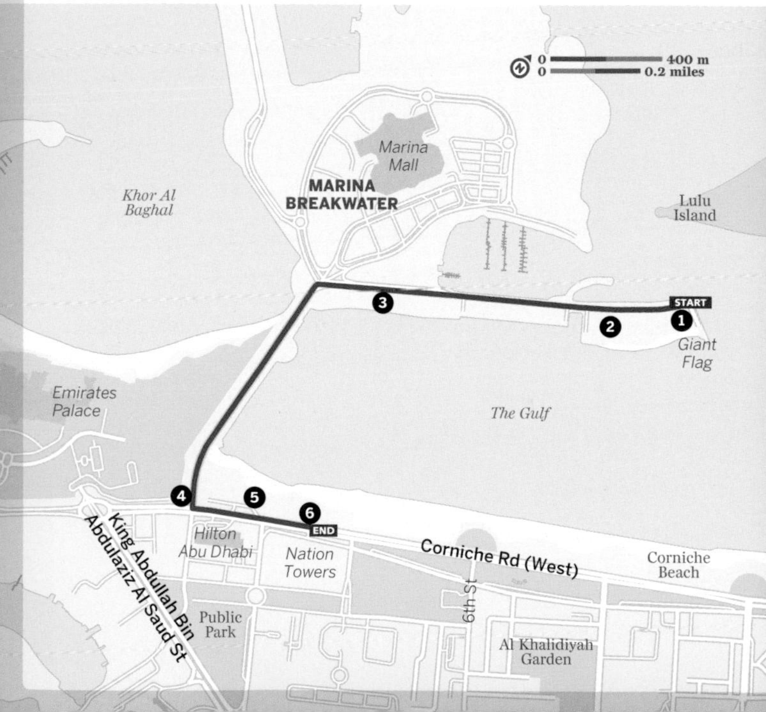

❶ Corniche History

At the exuberantly large UAE flagpole (p59) right at the tip of Breakwater, you'll have one of the best uninterrupted views in town of Abu Dhabi's Corniche skyscrapers. It's hard to believe now, but up until the 1970s that strip of coastline rimmed by towers was where all the dhows and bigger ships pulled into town, right onto the main beach.

❷ Glimpse into the Past

In the heritage village (p58), take a look at the *barasti* (palm-leaf) houses designed to catch the breeze through the palm frond uprights, the ox-drawn well without which settled life was impossible, and the ancient *falaj* (irrigation channel) system. Pop into the dusty museum before heading down to the beach where dhow hulls sit in the sand.

❸ Shisha Stop

Sunset must be soon so duck into **Hookah Lounge** (☎02 666 1179; www.pentainvestment.net; Breakwater Rd, opposite Marina Mall; 🕑9am-1am Mon-Sat, to midnight Sun) for a lemon and mint sundowner. With one of the very best views of night-time Abu Dhabi, the outside terrace at this highly popular shisha cafe is always teeming with appreciative smokers. Grab a seat on the water's edge and watch the glass-and-steel towers glinting in the last rays of light.

❹ Father of the Nation

The Constellation is a monumental artwork that takes centre stage inside the *Founder's Memorial* (p52) plaza, which pays tribute to Sheikh Zayed, the leader whose single-minded vision built the Abu Dhabi of today. Lit up dramatically at night, The Constellation provides some of the most phenomenal night photography opportunities in town.

❺ Seafood Dinner

Dig into fresh fish at **Vasco's** (☎02 681 1900; www.radissonblu.com/en/resort-abu-dhabi-corniche; Corniche Rd (West), Radisson Blu; mains Dhs80-189; 🕑noon-3.30pm & 7-11pm; 🍸). Loads of restaurants dish up great seafood in Abu Dhabi. The menu twist here is a sprinkling of Portuguese flavours, a reminder of the early influence in the region of the Portuguese, who were protecting their coastal interests.

❻ On the Best Bit of Beach

A bit further northeast along the Corniche's waterfront promenade, you'll find Asia De Cuba (p67), where Abu Dhabi's young and beautiful hang out for cocktails on an outdoor terrace (in cooler months) that trails right out onto the beach. The unruffled shoreline offers views of Breakwater and beyond with rainbow-lit silhouettes aplenty.

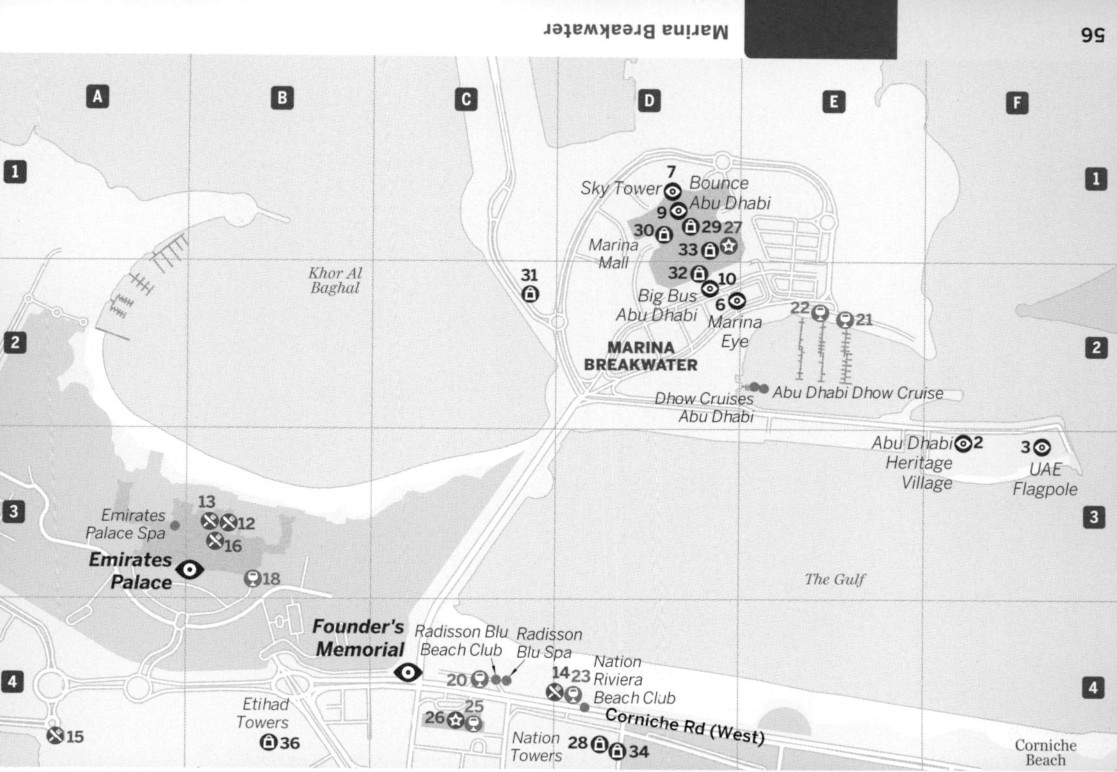
A
B
C
D
E
F
1
2
3
4
Khor Al Baghal
MARINA BREAKWATER
Sky Tower
Bounce Abu Dhabi
Marina Mall
Big Bus Abu Dhabi
Marina Eye
Dhow Cruises Abu Dhabi
Abu Dhabi Dhow Cruise
Abu Dhabi Heritage Village
UAE Flagpole
The Gulf
Emirates Palace Spa
Emirates Palace
Founder's Memorial
Radisson Blu Beach Club
Radisson Blu Spa
Nation Riviera Beach Club
Corniche Rd (West)
Etihad Towers
Nation Towers
Corniche Beach
2
3
6
7
9
10
12
13
14
15
16
18
20
21
22
23
25
26
27
28
29
30
31
32
33
34
36

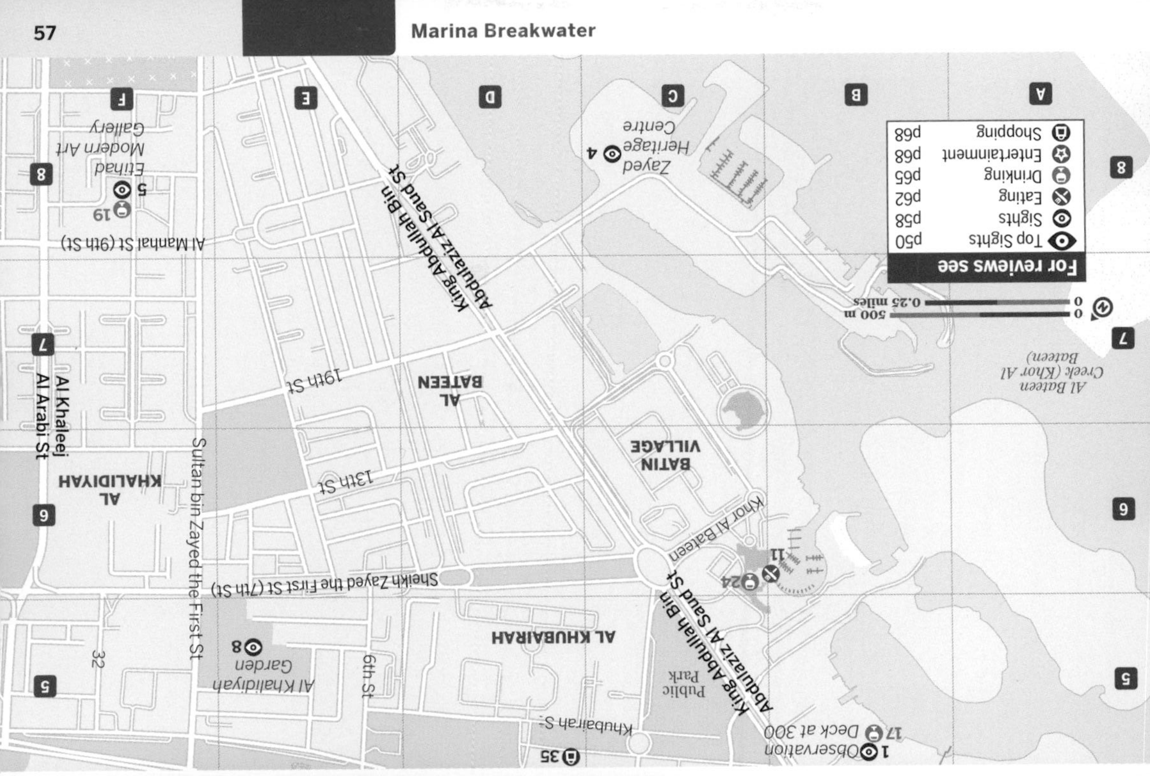
For reviews see
Top Sights p50
Sights p58
Eating p62
Drinking p65
Entertainment p68
Shopping p68
0 500 m
0 0.25 miles
1 Observation
17 Deck at 300
35
Khubairah St
AL KHUBAIRAH
Public Park
King Abdullah Bin Abdulaziz Al Saud St
24
11
Khor Al Bateen
BATIN VILLAGE
Al Bateen Creek (Khor Al Bateen)
Sheikh Zayed the First St (7th St)
6th St
Al Khalidiyah Garden
8
32
13th St
19th St
AL BATEEN
Zayed Heritage Centre
4
Sultan bin Zayed the First St
AL KHALIDIYAH
Al Khaleej Al Arabi St
Al Manhal St (9th St)
19
5
Etihad Modern Art Gallery
A
B
C
D
E
F
5
6
7
8

Sights

Observation Deck at 300

VIEWPOINT

1 MAP P56, B5

Ride the lift to the 74th floor (your ears may pop along the way) for panoramic views looking down on the skyscrapers and coastline below. The '300' refers to metres above sea level. The coffee shop here serves the highest high tea in the city. Admission includes Dhs50 towards food and drink. (02 811 5666; www.jumeirah.com; Corniche Rd (West), Tower 2, Jumeirah at Etihad Towers; entry Dhs95, high tea with/without champagne Dhs300/210; 10am-7pm)

Abu Dhabi Heritage Village

MUSEUM

2 MAP P56, F3

Although looking a bit worn and tired, this reconstructed village is one of the few places to get an insight into the pre-oil era of the United Arab Emirates. The walled complex includes all the main elements of traditional Gulf life: a fort to repel invaders from the sea, a souq to trade goats for dates with friendly neighbours and a mosque as a reminder of the central part that Islam plays in daily life. (www.torath.ae; Breakwater Rd; admission free; 9am-4pm Sat-Thu, 3.30-9pm Fri)

Abu Dhabi Heritage Village

The Bedouin Heart of Emirati Culture

The Abu Dhabi Heritage Village in Marina Breakwater recreates typical Bedouin lifestyle and culture, with goat-hair tents, palm-frond houses, a wind tower, *falaj* (irrigation canal) system and camel enclosure, to give you an idea of what Abu Dhabi was like before the oil boom swept that way of life away.

Today's Modern Bedouin

There are few Bedouin in the emirate of Abu Dhabi who live up to their name as true desert 'nomads' these days, but there are still communities who live a semi-traditional life on the fringes of the Empty Quarter. Their survival skills in a harsh terrain and their ability to adapt to changing circumstances are part of their enduring success. Most of today's Bedouin have modernised their existence with 4WD trucks (it's not unusual to find the camel travelling by truck), fodder from town and purified water from bowsers. All these features have limited the need to keep moving.

UAE Flagpole VIEWPOINT

3 MAP P56, F3

At 122m, this giant flagpole was the tallest free-standing flagpole in the world when it was constructed in 2001. It lost its title to the Raghadan Flagpole in Jordan in 2004 and is now a long way short of the world's tallest. You're not here to admire flagpole one-upmanship though; the promenade beneath the pole offers one of the best photo opportunities in Abu Dhabi for an uninterrupted view of the skyline. (Breakwater Rd; admission free)

Zayed Heritage Centre MUSEUM

4 MAP P56, C8

If you're into retro-tastic old museums, don't miss this eclectic, oddball collection of artefacts and personal memorabilia documenting the life of Sheikh Zayed, the founding father of the Emirates. Inside the main hall you'll find Zayed's favourite blue Mercedes, a beat-up Land Rover, his personal falcon clock, rifle and used cologne bottle. There are also plenty of weird and wonderful gifts given to the Sheikh by visiting dignitaries, including a stuffed leopard, an anaconda skin and a Guinness World Record-setting stamp mosaic. (02 665 9555; www.torath.ae; Bainunah St, Al Bateen; admission free; 8am-2.15pm Sun-Thu)

Etihad Modern Art Gallery GALLERY

5 MAP P56, F8

The brainchild of Emirati Khalid Seddiq Al Mutawa and German-Syrian Mohammed Khalil Ibrahim,

Beach Clubs

With 200m of perfect private pristine shoreline, speckled with plantation-style white pavilions and subtropical plantings, **Nation Riviera Beach Club** (Map p56, D4; 02 694 4780; www.nationrivierabeachclub.com; Corniche Rd (West); day use single/couple/family Sun-Thu Dhs160/265/370, Fri & Sat Dhs210/315/420; 6am-10pm) is one of Abu Dhabi's top beach club choices.

The **Radisson Blu Beach Club** (02 681 1900; www.radissonblu.com/en/resort-abu-dhabi-corniche; Corniche Rd (West); adult/couple/child Fri & Sat Dhs160/235/80, Sun-Thu Dhs105/170/80; 8am-8pm) occupies prime position at the western end of the Corniche. Set in landscaped gardens alongside a white-sand beach shaded by palm trees, the club offers three swimming pools, a gym and a cafe.

this Al Bateen villa hosts a rotating program of temporary exhibitions. It was the first privately funded gallery from the United Arab Emirates to host a large-scale exhibition in Berlin. In addition to fine art, there's an excellent bohemian cafe, Art House Cafe (p65). Exhibitions change monthly except in summer, when Art Souq showcases a wide variety of artists residing in the UAE. (02 621 0145; www.etihadmodernart.com; Villa 15, Al Huwelat St, Al Bateen; admission free; 10am-10pm Sat-Thu)

Marina Eye VIEWPOINT

6 MAP P56, D2

This observation big wheel sits rather incongruously in the Marina Mall car park but with the capsules reaching up to 60m at its highest point, it's a good option for panoramic city views. (www.freijwheels.com; Marina Mall; adult/child Dhs55/30; 11am-11pm Sun-Wed, to 1am Thu-Sat)

Sky Tower VIEWPOINT

7 MAP P56, D1

Marina Mall's observation tower has traditionally been the budget way to get 360-degree aerial views of the city, costing just the price of a coffee from the cafe at the top. The tower and cafe were closed for a refurbishment in 2018, with reopening pegged for some stage in 2019. (02 681 9009; Marina Mall; admission free; 9am-11pm)

Al Khalidiyah Garden PARK

8 MAP P56, E5

This garden is a good place for people-watching. Once the sun goes down Al Khalidiyah's paths are prime territory for strollers and joggers, while its fruit-shaped climbing frames in the playground area are a popular spot at weekends for local women and children – no boys over 10 years allowed. (Sheikh Zayed the

First St; admission free; ⏰8am-1am Mon-Sat, to midnight Sun)

Bounce Abu Dhabi TRAMPOLINE

9 MAP P56, D1

Kids of all ages can let off steam here. Fifty interconnected trampolines form the main stage (with an area reserved for wee ones, or 'mini-bouncers' as they call them) at this indoor park which also includes a zip line, 40m slide tube and 18m free-fall line for those who need an adrenaline rush. (☎04 3211 400; www.bounce.ae; Marina Mall; over/under 110cm height Dhs85/75; ⏰10am-10pm Sat-Wed, to midnight Thu & Fri)

Big Bus Abu Dhabi BUS

10 MAP P56, D2

This hop-on, hop-off bus tour with recorded commentary is an easy way to get the lie of the land. The main route loops past all the major sights, including Etihad Towers (p58), Sheikh Zayed Grand Mosque (p104) and the Louvre Abu Dhabi (p86). A second connecting route covers Yas Island. You can board the bus at any stop, but the nominal starting point is the Marina Mall (p70), with buses on the main route operating from here every 30 minutes between 9am and 5pm. (☎02 449 0026; www.bigbustours.com; 24hr adult/child Dhs260/166; ⏰9am-5pm)

View across Marina Breakwater

Eating

Tori No Su

JAPANESE $$

We like this place, located in Jumeirah in Etihad Towers (see 18 Map p56, B5), for its lighter noodle dishes such as spicy prawn yakisoba as well as the sushi and sashimi, but it's also known for its set lunch menus (Dhs150), which range from a seafood teppanyaki meal to a chicken katsu curry. (Corniche Rd (West), Jumeirah at Etihad Towers; mains & sushi Dhs40-165;)

Cho Gao Marina Walk

ASIAN $$

11 MAP P56, B6

The second branch of this much-loved restaurant (the original is downtown, see p41) has a desirable waterfront location with marina views, making it a standout choice. The pan-Asian menu draws on classic cooking from across the continent while the atmosphere is sociable and upbeat. (02 666 6888; www.abudhabi.intercontinental.com/cho-gao-marina-walk; Marina Walk, Intercontinental Hotel; mains Dhs50-180; noon-1am Sat-Wed, to 2am Fri & Sat; P)

Li Beirut

LEBANESE $$$

Ensconced in Jumeirah at Etihad Towers (see 17 Map p56, B5), a fine-dining Levantine feast awaits at Li Beirut. Scoop up Lebanese mezze classics of *moutabel* (purée of aubergine mixed with tahini, yoghurt and olive oil) and *muhammara* (red chilli and walnut dip) before moving on to rack of lamb encrusted with *zaatar* (a blend of spices that includes hyssop, sumac and sesame) or quail stuffed with *freekeh* (roasted green wheat). (02 811 5666; www.jumeirah.com; Corniche Rd (West), Jumeirah at Etihad Towers; mezze Dhs40-50, mains Dhs80-210, set menus from Dhs295; noon-3pm & 7pm-midnight Sep-May, dinner only Jul & Aug;)

Mezlai

EMIRATI $$$

12 MAP P56, B3

Meaning 'old door lock', Mezlai delivers a rare chance to enjoy traditional Emirati cuisine in an upmarket and airy Bedouin-tent-inspired atmosphere. The food is prepared from organic and locally sourced ingredients with favourites including *medfoun* (shoulder of lamb, cooked underground, wrapped in a banana leaf) and slow-cooked camel delicately flavoured with rose water and served with raisins and cashews. (02 690 7999; www.kempinski.com; Corniche Rd (West), Emirates Palace; mains Dhs128-318; 1-10.30pm;)

Sayad

SEAFOOD $$$

13 MAP P56, B3

Quite the contrast to the marble-gold-overload of the rest of the Emirates Palace, Sayad serves the city's finest seafood in a striking aquamarine setting. Head here for Parmesan-crusted turbot fillet served with quinoa in a velvety fish velouté, charcoaled oysters and beetroot risotto, or keep

Regional Menu Decoder

Downtown, Marina Breakwater and Al Bateen are three of the best districts to sample Abu Dhabi's Middle Eastern and regional Gulf foods, from cheap and cheerful mezze and kebab places to traditional Emirati stews lifted to fine-dining level.

Menus in the budget and midrange places tend to be novellas. To help you make your choice, here's a quick menu primer.

baba ganoush – smoked aubergine dip

fareed – lamb stew layered with flatbread

harees – a porridge-like stew made from cracked wheat and slow-cooked chicken or lamb

jasheed – minced baby shark with onions and spices

kibbeh – meat-filled cracked wheat croquettes

kunafeh – vermicelli-like pastry over a sweet-cheese base soaked in syrup

machboos – a casserole of meat or fish, rice and onions cooked in a spicy sauce

mandi – slow-roasted meat served with rice and chilli sauce

medfoun – shoulder of lamb, slow cooked in a banana leaf

shawarma – meat sliced off a spit and stuffed in a pocket of pita-type bread with chopped tomatoes and garnish

umm ali – dessert of filo pastry, butter, raisins and nuts baked in milk

things simple with the catch of the day served grilled, pan-seared, steamed or poached. (☎02 690 7999; www.kempinski.com; Corniche Rd (West), Emirates Palace; mains Dhs133-450; ⏰6.30-11.30pm; 📶)

Catch SEAFOOD $$$

14 MAP P56, D4

It's all about the seafood at this classy beachfront restaurant with the dining areas exuding Scandinavian minimalist style; all blonde wood, taupe and a dash of silver. Come for sushi plates to share with friends or for mains of grilled sea bream or miso-marinated salmon served with a lemon butter or saffron and yuzu butter sauce. (☎02 611 0909; www.catch.ae; Corniche Rd (West), Nation Riviera Beach Club; sushi Dhs59-79, mains Dhs139-219; ⏰noon-midnight)

Eating Etiquette

If you find yourself cross-legged on the timbers of a dhow with a communal plate in front of you, it's good to know a few tips about local protocol. Here are some of the main things to think about when dining the traditional Arab way:

- It's polite to be seen washing hands before eating.
- It's considered rude to eat with your legs stretched out.
- Don't take the best parts of the meat – if you're a guest, your host will be sure to lavish them on you. Strictly use only your right hand (the left hand is reserved for toileting) for eating or passing food.
- Discard unwanted food in a napkin rather than returning it to the communal plate.
- Leave a little food on your plate to avoid inviting famine. Feel free to pick your teeth after dinner.
- Don't leave the meal before coffee is served...
- ...but don't stay for too long afterwards. Most of the chatting is done before dinner, less during and almost none after!

Kamoon

MIDDLE EASTERN **$$$**

15 MAP P56, A4

Local families love this alcohol-free restaurant in the Khalidiya Palace for its traditional Middle Eastern menu. This is the place to try fish *sayadiya* (fish and rice cooked in a cumin-heavy sauce) and *kibbeh* (meat-filled cracked wheat croquettes) or do as the locals do and get a gang together so you can get stuck into the mezze for proper feasting. (02 657 0111; Corniche Rd (West), Khalidiya Palace Rayhaan; mezze Dhs37-65, mains Dhs87-162; noon-midnight)

Le Café

CAFE **$$$**

16 MAP P56, B3

From the Emirates Palace (p50) grand entrance, walk through its gold-edged central dome to Le Café in the back lobby for a cappuccino sprinkled with 24-carat gold flakes (Dhs73) or a camelccino (espresso with camel's milk, Dhs60). If that's not decadent enough, high tea here is an institution, featuring a selection of six sandwiches which balance both English and Arab traditions. (02 690 7999; www.emiratespalace.com; Corniche Rd (West), Emirates Palace; high tea for 2 people Dhs387-478; 6.30am-1am, high tea 2-6pm;)

Drinking

Ray's Bar

BAR

17 MAP P56, B5

For a prime perspective on Abu Dhabi's audacious architectural vision, let the lift whisk you up to this 62nd-floor bar at Jumeirah at Etihad Towers, which is all about cocktails and mocktails and skyscraper views. Arrive at sunset to be dazzled by the light bouncing off all the steel and glass. (02 811 5666; www.jumeirah.com; Corniche Rd (West), 5pm-2am;)

Hakkasan

COCKTAIL BAR

18 MAP P56, B3

All other cocktail bars may be dead to you once you've sipped a Pearl Sky (gin, rhubarb liqueur, yuzu, blackberry and lemon) or Sake Samurai (vodka, sake, mango, pineapple, cumin syrup and prosecco) cocktail (Dhs62) on Hakkasan's bar terrace while soaking up the views overlooking the vast, manicured grounds of the Emirates Palace. (02 690 7749; www.hakkasan.com; Corniche Rd (West), Emirates Palace; 3.30pm-1am;)

Art House Cafe

CAFE

19 MAP P56, F8

Beside, and connected to, Etihad Modern Art Gallery (p59), this artsy cafe, with its shaded patio scattered with tables and seating made from recycled oil barrels and fuel canisters, is a colourful bohemian hang-out. There's

Gold-decorated coffee and dessert at Le Café in Emirates Palace

Dhow Cruises

A couple of companies run dhow cruises from Breakwater's marina.

Dhow Cruises Abu Dhabi (Map p56, E2; ☎050 966 0720; www.dhowcruiseabudhabi.ae; Marina Breakwater; adult/child Dhs95/55; ⏲cruises 10.30am, 11.30am, 3.30pm & 4.30pm) has short, one-hour cruises with great views of Abu Dhabi's seafront along the way.

Abu Dhabi Dhow Cruise (Map p56, E2; ☎056 713 3703; www.abudhabidhowcruise.com; Marina Breakwater; dinner cruise adult/child Dhs250/200; ⏲7.30-10pm) offers dinner cruises with the lights of the city skyscrapers as your backdrop. The food is simple but includes fresh seafood. For an extra fee there is a pick-up service from major hotels. It also runs daytime speedboat sightseeing tours.

good coffee, excellent smoothies and breakfast plates as well as wraps, salads and burgers if you're peckish. (www.facebook.com/arthousecafead; Villa 15, Al Huwelat St, Al Bateen; ⏲9am-11.30pm Sun-Thu, 10am-midnight Fri & Sat; 📶)

Escape BAR

20 MAP P56, C4

Radisson Blu Beach Club's bar and shisha cafe – open to the public – sits on prime beachside real estate with outstanding skyline views to accompany slightly pricier puffing (shisha available noon to midnight, Dhs70 to Dhs80), as well as cocktails, beer (Dhs28 to Dhs47), wine (glass from Dhs38) and light bites. Happy hour is 5pm to 9pm, when some drink prices are slashed to Dhs26. (☎02 692 4344; www.radissonblu.com/en/resort-abu-dhabi-corniche; Corniche Rd (West), Radisson Blu Beach Club; ⏲9am-1am; 📶)

Yacht Gourmet Restaurant CAFE

21 MAP P56, E2

Serving a variety of fruit juices, mocktails and hot drinks, this simple cafe has a great outdoor terrace overlooking the marina for an evening of shisha and sipping *karak chai* (spicy tea). (☎02 222 2886; near Marina Mall, Marina Village; ⏲24hr; 📶)

Havana Café & Restaurant CAFE

22 MAP P56, E2

With one of the very best views of night-time Abu Dhabi, the outside terrace at this highly popular shisha cafe is always teeming with appreciative puffers, smokers and gurglers. The service is attentive despite the crowds and if you're peckish there's a great menu including multiple *fiteer* (Egyptian pastry) options. Good mocktails selection too. (02 681 0044; Corniche Rd (West); 9am-2am Sun-Thu, to 3am Fri & Sat;)

Asia De Cuba

LOUNGE

23 MAP P56, D4

Serious beachy vibes are yours, with a gin and *karkadai* (hibiscus) cocktail in hand. This chic open-air terrace, with the sand-front rimmed by cabana booths, is one of Abu Dhabi's top see-and-be-seen destinations. It's all about cocktails (Dhs50 to Dhs100) and fusion tapas plates of ceviche and bao buns. Glam up to get in. (02 699 3333; www.asiadecuba.com; Corniche Rd (West), Nation Riviera Beach Club; 3pm-midnight Sun-Wed, noon-2am Thu & Fri, noon-midnight Sat;)

Belgian Café

BAR

24 MAP P56, C6

The Arabian Peninsula is dire territory for hopheads, but the Belgian Café at the InterContinental boasts a satisfying suds selection, featuring five Belgian offers on draught and another 20 or so by the bottle. (02 666 6888; www.belgianbeercafe.com; King Abdullah Bin Abdulaziz Al Saud St, InterContinental Hotel; beers Dhs28-65; 4pm-1am Sat-Tue, to 2am Wed;)

Hemingway's

BAR

25 MAP P56, C4

An international/Tex-Mex/Irish cantina popular with long-term foreign residents, Hemingway's is the place to lounge in front of the

Dhow cruise

big screen with beer, chips (albeit nacho chips) and football. There's a DJ spinning nightly from 7pm and happy hour from 4pm to 8pm Sunday to Wednesday and Friday. (02 681 1900; Corniche Rd (West), Radisson Blu Hotel & Resort Abu Dhabi; noon-2am Sun-Wed, to 3am Thu & Fri;)

Entertainment

Jazz Bar & Dining

LIVE MUSIC

26 MAP P56, C4

Cool cats flock to this sophisticated supper club at the Radisson Blu that serves international cuisine in a modern art deco–inspired setting. But the venue is less about food and drink and more about music – a four-piece jazz band plays from 9.30pm to an audience of sagely nodding aficionados. It's ladies night Monday and Wednesday. (02 681 1900; Corniche Rd (West), Radisson Blu Hotel & Resort Abu Dhabi; mains Dhs105-155; 7pm-2am Sat-Wed, to 3am Thu & Fri;)

Vox Cinemas

CINEMA

27 MAP P56, D1

If you need to beat the heat, or the kids need a time-out, this ultracomfortable cinema has all the latest Hollywood and Bollywood blockbusters in 2D, 3D and 4D. Tickets can be booked online. (02 681 8464; www.uae.voxcinemas.com; Marina Mall; tickets Dhs35-150)

Shopping

Wafi Gourmet

FOOD

28 MAP P56, D4

Offering beautiful Medjool dates stuffed with pistachios, cashews, almonds or oranges; gorgeous marzipan, baklava and other Middle Eastern sweets; take-home bottles of rose water; and a full-service deli, bakery and restaurant, Wafi Gourmet is one-stop shopping for foodies looking to take home the taste of Arabia. (www.wafigourmet.com; Corniche Rd (West), Nation Galleria; 9am-midnight Mon-Sat, from 8.30am Sun)

Scarabee

GIFTS & SOUVENIRS

29 MAP P56, D1

From neon-coloured painted camel statues and wooden boxes engraved with Arabic calligraphy to salt and pepper shakers printed with Emirati figures, Scarabee has plenty of unique gift ideas. (02 681 2831; www.scarabee-uae.com; level 1, Marina Mall; 10am-10pm Sat-Wed, to midnight Thu & Fri)

Hind Al Oud

PERFUME

30 MAP P56, D1

Luxury fragrances, oils, home scents and skin care using the heady scents of *oud* (incense made from agarwood), rose, jasmine and saffron. (www.hindaloud.com; ground fl, Marina Mall; 10am-10pm Sat-Wed, to midnight Thu & Fri)

Abu Dhabi's Pearl Heritage

Take a walk along Abu Dhabi's Breakwater, and you'll come across a monument to an oyster – the mother of the pearl. Pearls are a common feature in Abu Dhabi because they formed a vital part of the region's former economy. In fact, for more than four centuries, the prosperity of the region was built on the collection and trading of these precious natural gems.

How Pearls are Created

Pearls are created when a grain of sand or grit enters the shell of an oyster, clam or mussel; the animal coats the intrusive irritant with a layer of nacre (mother-of-pearl) to make it smooth and less irksome. The longer the problem is nursed, the bigger it gets. Pearls are judged by the depth and quality of the lustre, and the perfection of the shape and the colour, which naturally ranges from peach to iron.

The Dangerous Work Behind the Beauty

Despite the beauty of the catch, pearling was an unglamorous and dangerous industry that entailed local 'divers' working with little more than a nose peg and a knife in shark-infested waters. They were hauled up with their bounty by 'pullers' working long and sun-baked shifts from June to October.

Boom & Bust

At the height of the industry, thousands of dhows were involved in pearling along the Trucial Coast, and loss of life was common.

A slump in the international pearl market in the 1930s alongside the development of the cultured pearl, pioneered in Japan in 1926, were the main reasons behind the demise of this back-breaking and risky work. A cultured pearl is usually created through the artificial injection of grit, or more often a plastic bead, into the shell of an oyster. The uniformity of the bead generally guarantees a more uniform pearl and it is created in a much shorter time.

Thankfully, soon after the pearling industry went bust, Abu Dhabi and neighbouring Emirates discovered oil – the black gold of the modern economy – but to this day the locals have a soft spot for the oyster and its precious cargo, and are proud of the pearling industry's role in their heritage.

Pearls are often used in jewellery here, adorning rings and necklaces in the gold shops of Madinat Zayed Gold Centre, and a dhow tour from the Eastern Mangroves Promenade is themed around Abu Dhabi's pearling history.

Miraj Islamic Centre

ARTS & CRAFTS

31 MAP P56, C2

Carpets, textiles, jewellery, sculpture, exquisite vases, marble inlay furniture and calligraphy are among the artworks from around the Islamic world displayed at this top-end gallery. Great for high-quality – albeit pricey – souvenir and gift shopping. (050 250 3950; www.mirajabudhabi.com; Villa 14, Marina Office Park; 9am-6pm)

Marina Mall

SHOPPING CENTRE

32 MAP P56, D2

In addition to more than 400 stores, this popular mall has plenty of entertainment choices, including a multiplex cinema, Bounce (p61), an indoor free-jumping centre for kids, the Emirates Bowling Village and the Marina Eye Ferris wheel (p60). (02 681 2310; www.marinamall.ae; 10am-10pm Sat-Wed, to midnight Thu & Fri;)

Maison Samira Maatouk

DRINKS

33 MAP P56, D1

Born in Lebanon in the '60s, Maison Samira Maatouk is a big name in Arabic coffee. At this kiosk in Marina Mall (p70), it sells its signature roasts. (www.maisonmaatouk.com; lower ground fl, Marina Mall; 10am-10pm Sat-Wed, to midnight Thu & Fri)

Marina Mall

Luxury Spa Treats

Emirates Palace Spa (Map p56, A3; ☎02 690 7978; www.kempinski.com; Corniche Rd (West), Emirates Palace; ⏲10am-11pm) is the ultimate indulgence. The Day of Gold ritual includes a 24-carat-gold facial, an application of gold from head to toe and a massage using gold shea butter. If you don't come out feeling like Tutankhamun's mummy, it won't be for want of trying. Prices on request (sit down first).

Rejuvenate jet-lagged limbs with a Thai massage or treat yourself to a spa package including body exfoliation, massage and deep-cleaning facial at the **Radisson Blu Spa** (Map p56, C4; ☎02 681 1900; www.radissonblu.com/en/resort-abu-dhabi-corniche; Corniche Rd (West); massages Dhs370-515; ⏲10am-10pm).

Nation Galleria SHOPPING CENTRE

34 MAP P56, D4

This small mall dedicated to the more extravagant end of the shopping market (the Lamborghini dealer is here) is worth a quick look if you're into decadent food gifts, as a huge branch of the celebrated Lebanese gourmet chain Wafi Gourmet is here. (☎02 681 8824; Corniche Rd (West), Nation Towers)

Organic Foods & Café FOOD & DRINKS

35 MAP P56, D5

This organic store inside Nation Galleria is Abu Dhabi's go-to for organic and natural food products and cosmetics. (www.organicfoodsandcafe.com; Corniche Rd (West), Nations Galleria; ⏲9am-11pm)

Avenue at Etihad Towers FASHION & ACCESSORIES

36 MAP P56, B4

Inside Etihad Towers' podium building, this mall is all about big-name designer boutiques. International names from Cartier to Versace all have a presence here as do more local names such as Emirati luxury chocolatier Manwa and Hind Al Oud. (☎800 384 4238; www.avenueatetihadtowers.ae; Corniche Rd (West), Jumeirah at Etihad Towers; ⏲hours vary)

Explore

Al Zahiyah & Al Maryah Island

Formerly known as 'Tourist Club Area' and still referred to by many as such today, Al Zahiyah is one of the city's oldest neighbourhoods. Today it's a hubbub of trading, chock-full of canteens, coffee houses and hotels. Al Maryah Island, by contrast, is a shiny new development that adds fine dining and cocktails as a feather in this area's cap.

The Short List

- ***Dai Pai Dong (p79)*** *Munching on dim sum at a terrace table along the Al Maryah Island Promenade.*
- ***Abu Dhabi Mall (p83)*** *Getting your food-gift shopping done with dates from Bateel.*
- ***Glo (p81)*** *Raising your glass to the lit-up skyline at this rooftop bar.*
- ***Coya (p79)*** *Sipping pisco as you sample high-class Peruvian cuisine.*
- ***Crust (p78)*** *Booking in for the fabled Friday brunch.*

Getting There & Around

🚌 Many bus routes stop at the city terminal. Bus 5 goes through here on its way to Abu Dhabi Global Market Square. The Big Bus tour bus stops outside Abu Dhabi Mall and links Al Zahiyah with Saadiyat Island.

🚖 There's a taxi stand outside Abu Dhabi Mall.

Al Zahiyah & Al Maryah Island Map on p76

Al Maryah Island

Top Sight

Abu Dhabi Global Market Square

At the heart of Al Maryah Island's urban development, Abu Dhabi Global Market Square (formerly called Sowwah Square) is on the cutting edge of modern town planning. Home to some of the city's most exciting construction and engineering projects, it's a glimpse of Abu Dhabi's ambitious vision for the future.

MAP P76, D5

Sowwah Sq

www.almaryahisland.ae

Al Falah St, Al Maryah Island

Birth of Abu Dhabi's New CBD

This area is flagged to become the city's new central business district, connected to Abu Dhabi Island by a new suspension bridge. The district offers a rare freehold opportunity for non-Emirati investors to build for the future, as part of Abu Dhabi's 2030 plan for sustainable development. Future plans include the US$1 billion Al Maryah Central Mall, pegged for opening at some stage in late 2019, turning an area that has already become a major dining and nightlife hub into one of the city's best shopping destinations.

Before the first phase of construction could even begin, 57 hectares of island first had to be elevated 14m above sea level.

Sustainable Features

The glinting sharp-edged buildings of Abu Dhabi Global Market Square have had smart sustainability features woven in to their architecture. With solar power, double-skin facades, recycled materials and active sun shading, they're designed to be energy efficient in extreme temperatures. The square's design has been awarded accreditation by LEED (Leadership in Energy and Environmental Design). The modern architecture itself is striking in places. Note the aerofoil shape of the **Rosewood Hotel** (02 813 5592; www.rosewoodhotels.com; Al Maryah Island; r from 600Dhs; P), its mushroom-shaped exterior shading, and the Galleria Mall's (pictured left; p83) steel-and-glass atrium.

A Walkable Solution

In a city where walking often seems to be a dirty word, the developments here have endeavoured to make the area more suitable for pedestrian movement. The manicured waterfront promenade (p77), and its cycle track, with its striking views over Al Zahiyah, is at the forefront of this commitment.

★ Top Tips

- The waterfront promenade is fully lit at night, great for evening strolling.
- For the best views of the Abu Dhabi Global Market Square area, walk across the suspension bridge, beside the Rosewood Hotel, back to Al Zahiyah.
- This area's becoming a major venue for annual events, with the waterfront promenade at the centre of things. On New Year's Eve expect concerts and great views of the fireworks, and at Christmas expect a full-on 'winter wonderland' experience for the kids.

Take a Break

For a way cheaper-than-average meal in this area, head to Biryani Pot (p78) for filling and exceedingly tasty big plates of biryani.

One of the top tables in town, Coya (p79), offers fine-dining Peruvian style.

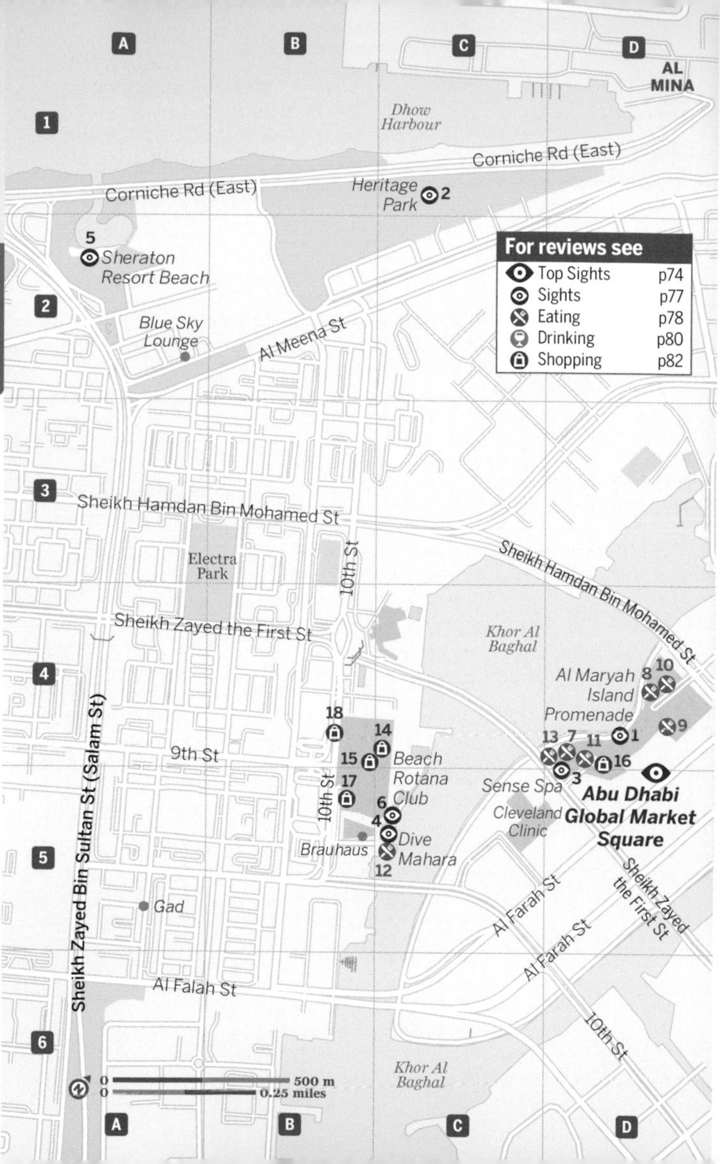

A
B
C
D
1
2
3
4
5
6
AL MINA
Dhow Harbour
Corniche Rd (East)
Corniche Rd (East)
Heritage Park 2
5 Sheraton Resort Beach
Blue Sky Lounge
Al Meena St
For reviews see
Top Sights p74
Sights p77
Eating p78
Drinking p80
Shopping p82
Sheikh Hamdan Bin Mohamed St
Sheikh Hamdan Bin Mohamed St
Electra Park
10th St
Sheikh Zayed the First St
Khor Al Baghal
Al Maryah Island Promenade
8
10
9
1
13
7
11
16
3
Sense Spa
Abu Dhabi Global Market Square
Cleveland Clinic
18
14
15
17
Beach Rotana Club
6
4
Dive Mahara
12
Brauhaus
9th St
10th St
Sheikh Zayed Bin Sultan St (Salam St)
Gad
Al Farah St
Al Farah St
Sheikh Zayed the First St
Al Falah St
10th St
Khor Al Baghal
0 500 m
0 0.25 miles

Sights

Al Maryah Island Promenade

WATERFRONT

1 MAP P76, D4

This 5.4km-long promenade bends gently round the western shore of Al Maryah Island and offers good views of Abu Dhabi and the busy channel of water in between. Backed by the outdoor terraces of the Galleria Mall's restaurants and cafes, it's a social, vibrant spot during the evenings of the cooler months. (Al Maryah Island; 24hr)

Heritage Park

PARK

2 MAP P76, C1

This attractive family park straddles both sides of the far eastern end of the Corniche, with great views of the traditional dhow harbour across the water in Al Mina. With fountains and faux grottoes, barbecue facilities and play areas, it is a popular picnic site at weekends. (24hr)

Sense Spa

SPA

3 MAP P76, D5

With nine treatment rooms, white leather lounges and traditional hammams, this is a temple of relaxation and therapy. It offers a masterclass in decadent design showcasing a marble soaking tub, bronze tiles, mist rooms, fibre-optic features and an infrared stone wall. Soak in a Cleopatra bath with goat's milk and the tub back home will never be the same again. (02-813 5537; www.

Beach Rotana Club (p78)

Friday Brunch

Clear your calendar on Friday. **Crust** (02 333 2222; www.fourseasons.com/abudhabi/dining/restaurants/crust; Four Seasons Abu Dhabi, Al Maryah Island; brunch buffet from Dhs330; 12.30-4pm Fri;) at the Four Seasons is one of Abu Dhabi's most social, indulgent Friday brunch extravaganzas. The brunch buffet includes freshly baked breads, decadent truffle mash, melt-in-your-mouth Wagyu bresaola, unbeatable crispy prawns and a seasonal rotation of desserts to die for. Don't expect the energy to see anything or go anywhere afterwards.

rosewoodhotels.com; Al Maryah Island, Rosewood Hotel; massages Dhs450-945, 30min milk bath Dhs310; 10am-10pm)

Dive Mahara DIVING

4 MAP P76, C5

This dive operator, based in the Beach Rotana Hotel's beach club, runs the full gamut of PADI dive qualifications as well as recreational dive trips out to the wrecks offshore for more experienced divers. You can also rent SUP-boards, kayaks and pedalos here. (02 697 9313; www.divemahara.com; 10th St, Beach Rotana Hotel; 2-dive trip Dhs420; 8am-7pm)

Sheraton Resort Beach SWIMMING

5 MAP P76, A2

The Sheraton's private lagoon with small beach and two pools makes a good spot for a lazy day of swimming and sunbathing. (www.marriott.com; Corniche (East), Sheraton Abu Dhabi Hotel & Resort; day access single/couple Sun-Thu from Dhs100/155, Fri & Sat Dhs130/210; 7am-10pm)

Beach Rotana Club SWIMMING

6 MAP P76, C5

With a small but pleasant beach, a grassy lawn, swimming pools and a wet bar-cafe, this club welcomes day visitors (though guests and members are prioritised if it gets crowded). There's an impressive view of the Al Maryah Island developments opposite. (02 697 9302; www.rotana.com; 10th St, Beach Rotana Hotel & Towers; single/couple/child Sun-Thu Dhs165/250/95, Fri & Sat Dhs230/335/95; 6am-11pm, pool 7am-10pm, beach 8am-sunset)

Eating

Biryani Pot INDIAN $

7 MAP P76, D4

Billed as gourmet Indian fast food, the 'Pot' does yummy biryanis all spiked with plenty of cardamom – including raved-about gluten-free organic versions with quinoa – as well as curries, tandoor grills and salads. The food-court setting isn't conducive to lingering unless you camp out on the terrace, which has water views. (www.biryanipot.ae; 2nd fl, Galleria Mall, Al Maryah Island; mains Dhs24-45; 10am-11pm Sat-Wed, to midnight Thu & Fri;)

Dai Pai Dong

CHINESE **$$**

All cosy alcoves surrounding an open kitchen, Dai Pai Dong's award-winning Chinese is where Asian foodies chase Cantonese roasted duck, spicy braised chicken and wok-fried beef tenderloin with green tea and cumquat mojitos. Once you've chowed down on its roasted pork buns or truffle and vegetable stuffed dumplings, you'll understand why Dai Pai Dong, located in the Rosewood Hotel (see **3** Map p76, D5), is known for its dim sum. (02 813 5552; www.rosewoodhotels.com; Rosewood Hotel, Al Maryah Island; mains Dhs48-194, dim sum Dhs30-55; noon-3pm & 6-11pm Sun-Wed, to midnight Thu & Fri;)

99 Sushi Bar

SUSHI **$$**

8 MAP P76, D4

All your *maki*, *gunkan* and *nigiri* sushi cravings are satisfied at this outpost of Spain's premier Japanese restaurant. There are plentiful twists on traditional sushi flavours to get stuck into including squid and truffle *gunkan* and meat *wagyu maki*, though we're happy gulping down as many roasted eel *nigiri* rolls as we can. (02 672 3333; www.99sushibar.com; Galleria Mall, Al Maryah Island; sushi Dhs50-135; noon-3.30pm & 7-11.30pm Sun-Wed, to 12.30am Thu & Fri;)

Coya

PERUVIAN **$$$**

9 MAP P76, D4

The contemporary Peruvian cuisine with its flavour-fusion of Latin American and Asian is a tastebud sensation. Dig into the menu of sharing plates featuring traditional ceviche, Peruvian sashimi and tacos (we recommend the *cangrejo* stuffed with crab and wasabi) and you'll see what the fuss is about. Impressive waterfront views add a luxurious feel: perfect for a romantic night out. (02 306 7000; www.coyarestaurant.com; Galleria Mall, Al Maryah Island; small plates Dhs50-124, mains Dhs98-980; noon-5pm Sun-Thu, 12.30-4pm Fri, to 5.30pm Sat, plus 7pm-12.30am daily)

Butcher & Still

STEAK **$$$**

10 MAP P76, D4

How good is this 1920s Chicago–inspired steakhouse at Four Seasons Abu Dhabi? We don't have enough space to tell you. American chef Marshall Roth sources his meat from the Temple Grandin–designed Creekstone Farms in Kansas (USA); when paired with his from-scratch béchamel creamed spinach, you have a perfectly executed classic combination. (02 333 2444; www.fourseasons.com/abudhabi/dining/restaurants/butcher_and_still; Four Seasons Abu Dhabi, Al Maryah Island; steak Dhs280-490; 6pm-midnight;)

Local Eats

The bright red neon lights of **Gad** (Map p76, A5; off Al Falah St; shawarma & sandwiches Dhs4-15, mains Dhs12-50; 7am-1am;) are a beacon for meals on the cheap. This Egyptian street-food chain (famed in its home country) is all about budget Middle Eastern street food. This is where you come for sandwiches of falafel, *fuul* (mashed fava bean paste; we recommend the Alexandrian *fuul*), and meat shawarmas (meat sliced off a spit and stuffed in a pocket of pita-type bread with chopped tomatoes and garnish).

Zuma

JAPANESE $$$

11 MAP P76, D4

The summit of Japanese cuisine in Abu Dhabi. Book ahead to enjoy the superb sushi and sashimi, the signature miso-marinated black cod or a hunk of meat cooked to perfection on the robata grill. Alcohol served (sake, finely curated cocktails and Hitachino, one of Japan's best craft beers). The beautiful bar, fashioned from striking Indonesian teak, is buzzy to boot. (02 401 5900; www.zumarestaurant.com; Galleria at Maryah Island, Al Maryah Island; mains Dhs120-358; noon-3.30pm & 7pm-midnight Sat-Wed, to 1am Thu & Fri;)

Finz

SEAFOOD $$$

12 MAP P76, C5

Amble down the jetty to this A-frame with terraces above the sea and enjoy some of the finest seafood in town. Whether it's chargrilled, steamed or baked, the results are invariably delicious in this classic of Abu Dhabi's seafood scene. Whole sea bass baked in salt for two remains a staple, but newer, surprisingly paired dishes are worth considering (scallops with short ribs etc). (02 697 9011; www.rotana.com; 10th St, Beach Rotana Hotel; mains Dhs97-384; 6-11.30pm Tue-Fri & Sun, plus 12.30-3.30pm Thu & Fri, 12.30-11.30pm Sat;)

Roberto's

ITALIAN $$$

13 MAP P76, D4

The pastas and risottos are already something of a legend around the capital, and even the most seemingly simple dishes are packed with rich and deep flavours. Roberto's Ravioli is our pick on the menu. The signature cocktails are worth staying for, best enjoyed on the outdoor terrace with waterside city views. (02 627 9009; www.robertos.ae; Galleria Mall, Al Maryah Island; mains Dhs95-249; noon-3am)

Drinking

Dragon's Tooth

COCKTAIL BAR

Just the coolest speakeasy-style bar in town. Walk through the front door of Dai Pai Dong and head left to stumble into this secret drinking den, located in the Rosewood Hotel (see 3 Map p76, D5). It's all leather and brass, which seems to have fallen out of the 1920s. Cocktails are super creative. Our favourite is the Black Panda with rum, amaretto, activated charcoal, and blackberry and rosemary syrup. (www.rosewoodhotels.com; Dai Pai Dong restaurant, Rosewood Hotel, Al Maryah Island; 6pm-1am Sat-Wed, to 2am Thu & Fri)

Glo ROOFTOP BAR

The rooftop bar at the Rosewood hotel (see 3 Map p76, D5) is one of our top choices for a chilled-out night. Lounge with friends while drinking wine and taking in Abu Dhabi's skyline. Tuesday is ladies night, with free Prosecco between 6pm and 9pm. (02 813 5550; www.rosewoodhotels.com; Rosewood Hotel, Al Maryah Island; noon-1am Oct-May;)

Zsa Zsa COCKTAIL BAR

Tucked away in an inconspicuous corner of the main lobby (see 10 Map p76, D4), this bar is inspired by vivacious Hungarian actress Zsa Zsa Gabor. Her stylish but flamboyant reputation becomes apparent as you step through the boldly patterned screen doorway and on to the brightly lit monochrome runway-style floor. It's a great spot for an aperitif or two. (02 333 2222; www.fourseasons.com/abudhabi/dining/lounges/zsa_zsa; Four Seasons Abu Dhabi, Al Maryah Island; 5pm-1am Sat-Wed, from 4pm Thu & Fri)

Zsa Zsa

Eclipse Terrace Lounge ROOFTOP BAR

Poolside Eclipse, in the Four Seasons Abu Dhabi (see 10 Map p76, D4), is a worthy spot to enjoy stunning views over the water and rooftops of the city. During the day it has a laid-back and relaxed vibe. The lounge comes alive for sundowners and with atmospheric chill-out tunes from the DJ as the understated but well-heeled pre-dinner crowd arrive. (02 333 2222; www.fourseasons.com; 3rd fl, Four Seasons Abu Dhabi, Al Maryah Island; noon-8pm)

Al Meylas LOUNGE

The Four Season's lobby lounge (see 10 Map p76, D4) comes into its own during the cooler months when you can sit outside with a drink on the terrace and take in the city skyline as the sun goes down. Come between 3pm and 6pm for afternoon tea (from Dhs150) with melt-in-your-mouth buttery scones and a glass of bubbles. (02 333 2222; www.fourseasons.com; Four Seasons Abu Dhabi, Al Maryah Island; 9am-1am)

La Cava WINE BAR

Saunter down a dramatic candlelit staircase to this cellar-like hideaway in the Rosewood Hotel (see 3 Map p76, D5), probably Abu Dhabi's best destination for oenophiles in need. More than 1000 wine labels await, a handful of which are available by the glass (give Ixsir Altitudes Red from Lebanon a shot). Pair with the all-you-can-eat buffet of gourmet Spanish tapas, cheeses and desserts. (02 813 5550; www.rosewoodhotels.com/en/abu-dhabi/dining/la-cava; Rosewood Hotel, Al Maryah Island; 5pm-1am;)

Butcher & Still COCKTAIL BAR

A connoisseur's cocktail bar, Butcher & Still, in the Four Seasons Hotel (see 10 Map p76, D4) has a black marble bar, hardwood features and leather everywhere to pad the elbows. Smoked Manhattans and other creative Prohibition-era tipples, often made with house-mixed bitters, syrups and tinctures, dominate. Selected cocktails are shaken in an antique Tanqueray No 10 Imperial Shaker, one of only five in the world. (www.fourseasons.com/abudhabi/dining/restaurants/butcher_and_still; Four Seasons Hotel, Al Maryah Island; cocktails Dhs55-100; 4pm-2am;)

Shopping

Spirit of Dubai PERFUME

14 MAP P76, C4

Luxury UAE fragrance range based on Emirati culture and heritage. *Oud* (incense made from agarwood), saffron, bergamot, frankincense and rose are the key notes in the heady scents. (www.thespiritofdubai.com; 10th St, 1st fl, Abu Dhabi Mall; 10am-10pm)

Bateel

FOOD

15 MAP P76, B4

Gourmet date products for you to take a little taste of the Gulf home. Choose from chocolate-covered dates or the little morsels stuffed with candied peel. (02 645 2121; www.bateel.com; 10th St, Abu Dhabi Mall; 10am-10pm)

Galleria Mall

SHOPPING CENTRE

16 MAP P76, D4

Shopping for those with deep pockets: this flashy mall with its cathedral-high ceilings and sculptural roof is all about international couture brands (think Prada and Dior). With a swag of dining and drinking options, it's also a nightlife hub. Many of the restaurant-bars here are positioned on the waterfront promenade side, so good outdoor socialising opportunities (in cooler months) abound. (02 616 6999; www.thegalleria.ae; Al Falah St, Al Maryah Island; 10am-10pm Sat-Wed, to midnight Thu, noon-midnight Fri;)

Abu Dhabi Mall

SHOPPING CENTRE

17 MAP P76, B5

Al Zahiyah's major shopping destination has plenty of international brand-names among its 200 shops, a **cinema** (02 645 8988; https://uae.voxcinemas.com; 10th St, 3rd fl; tickets Dhs35-55) and kids entertainment area, a big **hypermarket** (02 645 9777; www.abudhabicoop.com/english; 10th St, ground fl; 8am-midnight) and cafes. (02 645 4858; www.abudhabi-mall.com; 10th St; 10am-10pm Sat-Wed, to 11pm Thu & Fri;)

Beer Haunts

Beer fans unite. The comfy **Brauhaus** (Map p76, B5; www.rotana.com; 10th St, Beach Rotana Hotel; 3pm-1am Sun-Thu, noon-1am Fri & Sat;) bar – all dark wood, traditional interior inside and plentiful outdoor seating – in the Beach Rotana Hotel, is where you go to sup on Löwenbräu and other German beers.

For sports and beer, **Blue Sky Lounge** (Map p76, A2; www.tsogosun.com; Al Meena St, Southern Sun Abu Dhabi; 3pm-3am Sun-Thu, from noon Fri & Sat;) is a bright, modern bar with all the big screens you need to watch a game, and a friendly atmosphere. Tuesday is quiz night if you feel like being social.

Khalifa Centre

GIFTS & SOUVENIRS

18 MAP P76, B4

For a wide range of souvenirs (shisha pipes, camel-bone boxes, stuffed leather camels, carpets and cushion covers), head to the Khalifa Centre, across the road from the Abu Dhabi Mall, where you'll find a dozen independent stores, mostly run by the expat Indian community, selling handicrafts and carpets. (10th St; 10am-1pm & 4-10pm Sat-Thu, 4-10pm Fri)

Explore

Al Mina & Saadiyat Island

Saadiyat Island, with the Louvre Abu Dhabi centre-stage, is a dramatic statement of the city's push to become the cultural capital of the Gulf while Al Mina's dhow harbour and ragtag souqs are a glimpse of old Abu Dhabi. Check out the fishing heritage, marvel at global history in the Louvre, then digest it all on Saadiyat's white sand.

The Short List

- ***Louvre Abu Dhabi (p86)*** *Meandering through the entirety of human artistic heritage.*
- ***Saadiyat Public Beach (p94)*** *Lounging on the city's nicest strip of public sand.*
- ***Al Mina Fish Market (p91)*** *Digging into fresh seafood from the market hall in one of the attached fish-grill canteens.*
- ***Dhow Harbour (p94)*** *Strolling the harbour front for views of creaky fishing dhows.*
- ***Beach House (p97)*** *Enjoying a sunset cocktail with views out to the rolling coastal dunes.*

Getting There & Around

The 54 bus travels between the dhow harbour and Sheikh Zayed Grand Mosque. Bus 44 travels the same route but to the fruit and vegetable market. The 94 service travels between Sheikh Zayed Grand Mosque and the Louvre Abu Dhabi. The Big Bus tour bus stops at the Louvre Abu Dhabi.

Al Mina & Saadiyat Island Map on p92

Saadiyat Island Public Beach (p94) URBANMYTH/ALAMY STOCK PHOTO ©

Top Sight

Louvre Abu Dhabi

The Louvre Abu Dhabi is the city's new cultural icon. A celebration of humanity's artistic achievements, the galleries of this fabulous museum take you on a dazzling journey through the wealth of global cultural heritage. From eerily beautiful artefacts of the Neolithic era to Ai Weiwei's 2016 'Fountain of Light', this is human history told through art. Don't miss it.

MAP P92, C3

www.louvreabudhabi.ae

Saadiyat Island

adult/aged 13-22yr/under 13yr Dhs63/31/free

10am-8pm Sat & Sun, Tue & Wed, to 10am Thu & Fri

Humanity's Story

Turning the tables on a typical museum experience, where collections are grouped together by civilisation or country, the Louvre Abu Dhabi has curated its galleries into themes that instead walk you through the different eras of history, starting from prehistory in the Great Vestibule and then tracing the rise and advancement of civilisation in the following 12 galleries. This means you encounter unexpectedly beautiful juxtapositions. In Gallery Three 'Civilisations and Empires', a glazed brick Persian archer dating from the Achaemenid Empire sits behind a bronze winged dragon from northern China, and a Kushan Empire bodhisattva statue from Pakistan is displayed near a case containing masks and statuettes from Mexico's Teotihuacan culture. In Galley Eight 'The Magnificence of The Court', French and Italian 17th-century oil paintings depicting royalty grace the walls while a central case displays the bronze head of an Edo Culture king from Nigeria. It's a revolution in museum curation that celebrates the connections and similarities across humanity that transcend countries and borders.

Architecture

The building, with its 7500-ton silver dome that seems to hover above the walls, was designed by Pritzker Prize–winning architect Jean Nouvel. The dome's structure is made from multiple layers of metal perforated into a tapestry of 7850 stars, which (taking inspiration from how date palms filter the effects of bright sunlight with their broad leaves) creates a dappled light effect underneath. After you've finished your tour of the galleries, a door into the plaza takes you under the dome to admire it close up. Here, the turquoise waters of the Gulf lap straight up to the plaza walkways and stairs while the geometric light patterns play on the floors and surrounding walls on buildings.

★ Top Tips

- Make sure you have left enough time in your schedule to explore (two hours if you're just browsing, longer if you've got an interest in art, anthropology, archaeology or history).
- Come early or late to try to avoid the school groups and tour buses.
- Ninety-minute tours (adult/child Dhs50/30) highlighting the museum's masterpieces are offered at 11am and 2pm daily in English and at 5pm on Friday in Arabic and French.

Take a Break

The Museum Cafe (p96) offers full bistro-style meals and lighter bites such as packaged sandwiches as well as excellent coffee.

If you're heading to the beach afterwards, pull in to the Beach House (p97) along the way for sunny Mediterranean flavours before you hit the sand.

Gallery Highlights

The permanent collection holds so many highlights for both history and art fans that it's difficult to pick out only a few.

Gallery One

In Gallery One ('The First Villages') don't miss Jordan's 7th Millennium BC Ain Ghazal statue, thought to be one of the first artistic representations of humans.

A display case to the side features smaller treasures. Of these, a 3rd Millennium BC statue, from the Oxus Civilisation, of a Bactrian princess wearing an intricately detailed woollen garment is one of the most beautiful pieces. Note too the two-headed plank statuette (also dating to the 3rd Millennium BC) from Cyprus, with its bold geometric designs.

Gallery Two

Gallery Two ('The First Great Powers') is dominated by statues and stonework from the ancient civilisations of Egypt, Mesopotamia and northern China. Don't miss the side cases here that display ceramic pieces from the United Arab Emirates' own Um Al Nar culture which carried out trade with the Sumerian and Akadian cities in Mesopotamia as well as the cities of the Indus Valley.

The major highlight of Gallery Two is the imposing black statue of Gudea, prince of Laqash from Iraq's neo-Summerian era.

Gallery Three

An elegant sculpture of a female sphinx from Greece (600-500 BC) welcomes you to Gallery Three

Gallery 2 ('The First Great Powers')

('Civilisations and Empires'). Here, admire 'The Orator', a marble statue from Ancient Rome. It stands near a finely detailed schist statue depicting a bodhisattva from Gandhara in modern-day Pakistan.

Gallery Four

In Gallery Four ('Universal Religions') an intricately decorated 2nd-century Buddhist stupa plaque from India is given centre stage.

Also look out for the fine 1st-century bronze dancing Shiva from Tamil Nadu's (in India) Choia Kingdom and the golden-toned statue of Sho-Kannon the bodhisattva of compassion from Japan.

Gallery Five & Six

The vast network of trade routes that linked cultures from Europe to Asia and Africa are explored in Gallery Five ('Asian Trade Routes') and Gallery Six ('From the Mediterranean to the Atlantic').

Don't miss the delightful painted terracotta Bactrian camel from China's Tang Dynasty, the intricately engraved bone-on-wood casket from Byzantine Constantinople and the monumental bronze lion from Spain.

Gallery Seven

The 15th-century ceramic bust of St Peter of Verona by Italian Renaissance sculptor Andrea della Robbia is one of the most stunning works in Gallery Seven ('The World in Perspective').

Gallery Eight

In Gallery Eight ('The Magnificence of the Court') the standout piece is the 'Horses of the Sun' sculpture, originally created for the Palace of Versailles. Make sure to check out the smaller scale objects here too. The equestrian statue of Spain's King Philip V and the display cases of bronze and brass heads from Nigeria's Edo Culture are particularly beautiful.

Galleries Nine & 10

In Gallery Nine ('A New Art of Living') and Gallery 10 ('A Modern World?') cases displaying wooden ceremonial statuettes from Papua New Guinea and Gabon make a striking contrast with the refined 18th- and 19th-century paintings on the walls. Look out for Osman Hamdi Bey's 'Young Emir Studying' and Paul Gauguin's 'Children Wrestling'.

Galleries 11 & 12

For modern art fans, Galleries 11 ('Challenging Modernity') and 12 ('A Global Stage') hold a roll-call of the 20th century's most famous names in art and the most prominent names working in art today.

Among the renowned pieces here are Mondrian's 'Composition with Blue, Red, Yellow and Black', Picasso's 'Portrait of a Woman' and Ai Weiwei's 'Fountain of Light' sculpture.

Walking Tour

Markets of Al Mina

They may be constructed of concrete rather than barasti (palm fronds) and air-conditioned rather than piled along dusty alleyways, but Al Mina's modern market stalls are every bit as traditional in spirit as their ancient predecessors. Visitors are welcome, as long as they don't interfere with the important business of making a sale!

Walk Facts

Start Carpet Souq

End Dhow harbour

Length 2.5km; 40 minutes

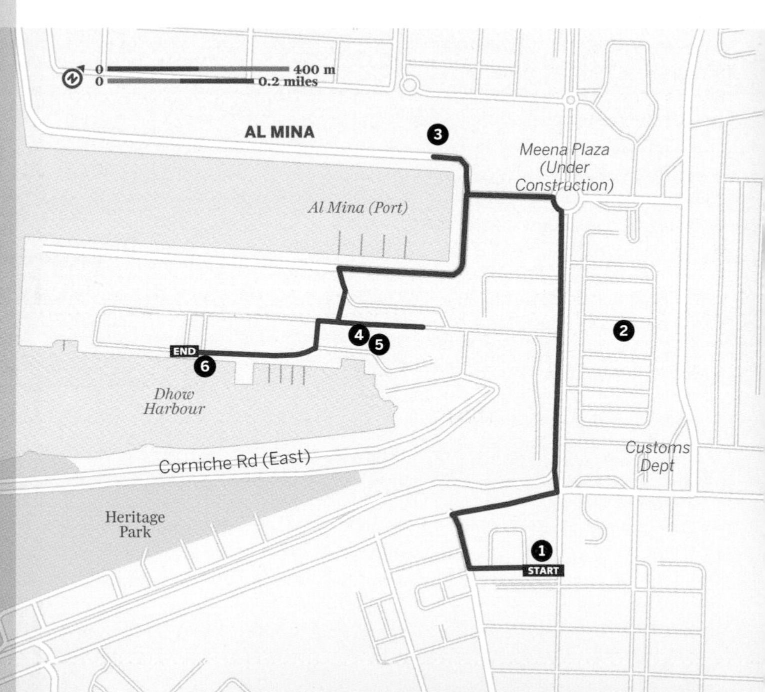

❶ A Pile of Polyester

Forget notions of Oriental bazaars selling fine Persian silk carpets. The **Carpet Souq** (Al Mina; ⏰9am-11pm) in Al Mina is where the average Gulf family comes to buy a washable polyester carpet for the *majlis* (reception room), a new portable prayer rug or a set of cushions upholstered in traditional Bedouin geometric patterns of red, black and green.

❷ Date Heaven

Stock up on your vitamin C intake with a few purchases in the **Fruit & Vegetable Market** (p99). Produce from across the Middle East (and beyond) finds its way to this large complex of stalls. This is where you come to learn date 101 amid the shops selling all the different varieties of this humble fruit.

❸ All the Things You Never Knew You Wanted

The cramped collection of stalls at the **Iranian Souq** (Al Mina; ⏰7am-midnight) are piled high with aluminium cooking pots large enough to cook for a family of 14, brooms, ropes, melamine trays sporting European floral designs, Chinese plastic decorations, wicker-ware, thermoses and modern copper coffee pots. Look out for a few local crafts like rice mats (around Dh40).

❹ Catch of the Day

Never mind the prospect of lots of tasty seafood, the fish market is a visual feast of colour, texture and design. Rhythmical arrangements of prawns, orange-spotted trevally, blue-shelled crabs, red snappers, pink Sultan Ibrahims and a host of unlikely edibles from the sea straddle the ice bars of this large **fish market** (Dhow Harbour, Al Mina; ⏰7am-10pm).

❺ Try Something Fishy

For a simple, as-fresh-as-it-gets meal, buy your fish and have it gutted and prepared direct at the market, then head to one of the attached canteens to have it cooked up. For local eating, rubbing shoulders with harbour-hands and traders, beeline to tiny Indian restaurant **Virona** (Fish Market, Al Mina; set lunch Dhs7-18; ⏰11am-3pm), at the back, which cooks up set plates of biryani and dahl (lentils).

❻ From Dhow to Dinner Plate

After dinner, see where your fish came from. Take a walk along the **dhow harbour** (p94) crammed full of creaky wooden boats that still make up the local fishing fleet. It's busiest early in the morning but prettiest at sunset, with the bobbing vessels tied at dock back-dropped by high-rises glowing in the ebbing light.

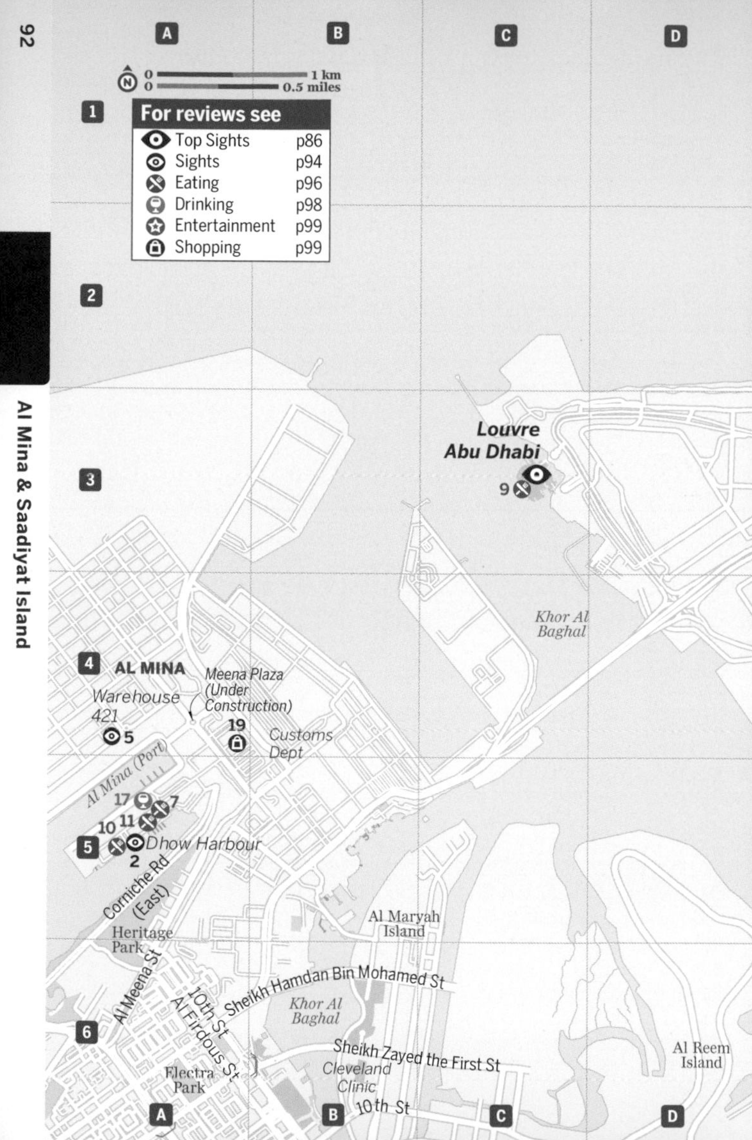

A
B
C
D
1
2
3
4
5
6
0 1 km
0 0.5 miles
For reviews see
Top Sights p86
Sights p94
Eating p96
Drinking p98
Entertainment p99
Shopping p99
Louvre Abu Dhabi
9
Khor Al Baghal
AL MINA
Meena Plaza (Under Construction)
Warehouse 421
5
19
Customs Dept
Al Mina (Port)
17
7
11
10
2
Dhow Harbour
Corniche Rd (East)
Heritage Park
Al Maryah Island
Al Meena St
10th St
Al Firdous St
Sheikh Hamdan Bin Mohamed St
Khor Al Baghal
Sheikh Zayed the First St
Cleveland Clinic
Electra Park
10th St
Al Reem Island

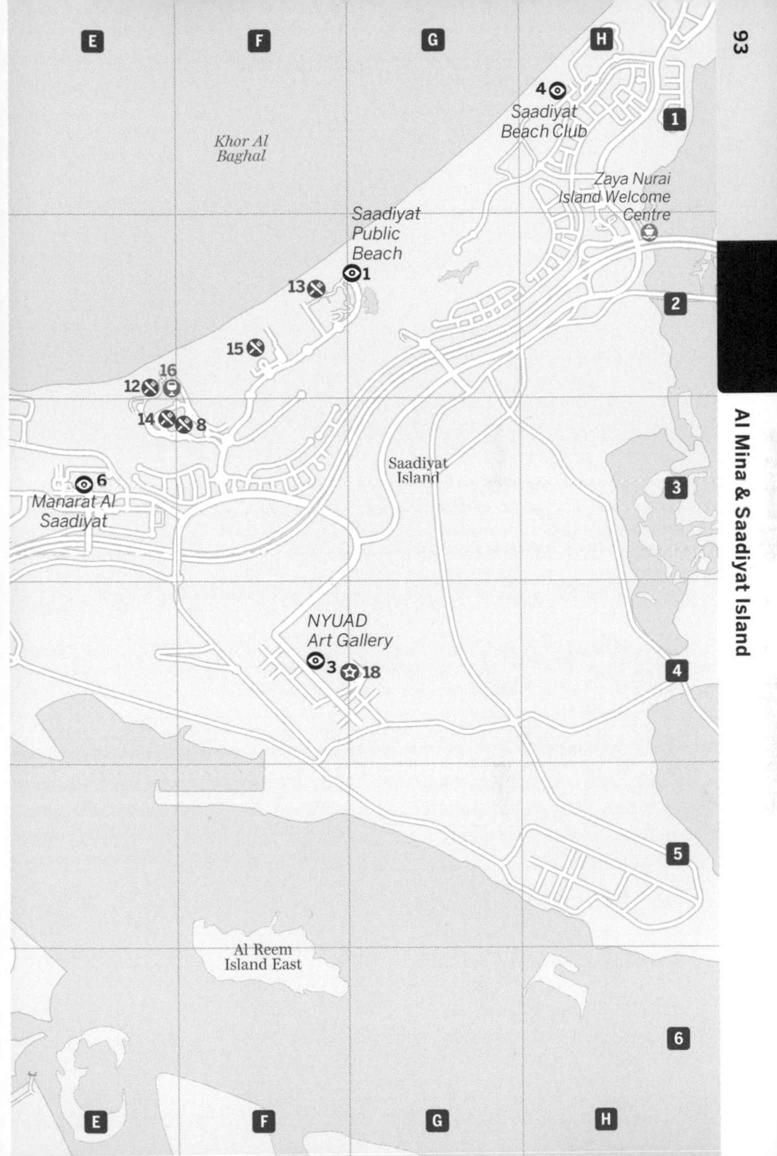
E
F
G
H
1
2
3
4
5
6
Khor Al Baghal
4
Saadiyat Beach Club
Zaya Nurai Island Welcome Centre
Saadiyat Public Beach
1
13
15
16
12
14
8
6
Manarat Al Saadiyat
Saadiyat Island
NYUAD Art Gallery
3
18
Al Reem Island East

Sights

Saadiyat Public Beach BEACH

1 MAP P92, G2

By far Abu Dhabi's nicest public beach. A boardwalk leads through a protected zone of coastal vegetation, home to nesting turtles, to this prime slice of powdery white beach on the northwest coast of Saadiyat Island (neighbouring the Park Hyatt resort). There's a lifeguard until sunset and a cafe, though you're able to bring in your own picnic supplies (no alcohol allowed). Towel rental is Dhs10 and sun-loungers with umbrella are Dhs25 weekdays and Dhs50 Friday and Saturday. (www.bakeuae.com; Saadiyat Island; adult/child Dhs25/15; 8am-8pm)

Dhow Harbour HARBOUR

2 MAP P92, A5

There's something fascinating about sitting by the harbour watching the dhows (traditional wooden cargo boats) slip off to sea. At any time of day, there's work going on as fishers mend their nets, pile up lobster pots, hang out colourful sarongs to dry, unload fish and congregate for communal chats. As you survey the resting dhows strung together five abreast, you can almost forget Abu Dhabi's modern backdrop as its ancient past as a fishing village is revealed. (Al Mina)

NYUAD Art Gallery GALLERY

3 MAP P92, F4

If you're a fan of cutting-edge art, come visit the temporary art exhibitions held here, in the art gallery of New York University's Abu Dhabi campus. The focus is on bringing current regional and international issues to the fore and promoting the best contemporary artists working today. Check the website to see what's on while you're in town. (www.nyuad-artgallery.org; NYU Abu Dhabi Campus; admission free; noon-8pm Mon-Sat during exhibitions)

Saadiyat Beach Club BEACH

4 MAP P92, H1

This luxurious, exclusive beach club, spa and fitness centre is open to day visitors and offers an expanse of pristine beach with plenty of sun-loungers and umbrellas, a beautiful pool if seawater isn't your thing, a workout room offering yoga classes, plus a handful of upmarket bars and cafes. Protected hawksbill turtles nest along the coast and the occasional school of dolphins is spotted in the turquoise waters. (02 656 3500; www.saadiyatbeachclub.ae; couple/adult/child Sun-Thu Dhs295/210/85, Fri & Sat Dhs445/320/125; beach 9am-sunset, other facilities to 8pm)

Warehouse 421 ARTS CENTRE

5 MAP P92, A4

In a former port warehouse, this contemporary arts centre and gallery hosts temporary exhibitions showcasing the UAE's art, design and creative scenes. There's usually one or two small exhibitions running. The website lists what's on. There's also a program of creative workshops and film screenings in winter. It's a good bet for checking out the latest in cutting-edge Abu Dhabi culture. Look for the 18m-long cast-iron ship out the front. (www.warehouse421.ae; Al Mina; admission free; ⏲10am-8pm Tue-Sun)

Manarat Al Saadiyat — ARTS CENTRE

Housed in a postmodern building with an eye-catching honeycomb mantle, Manarat Al Saadiyat ('place of enlightenment') hosts regular art courses and workshops

The Ongoing Saga of Saadiyat Cultural District

The **Louvre Abu Dhabi** (p86) is the first museum in a grand plan to transform a corner of Saadiyat Island into the world's biggest culture-focused district. Boldly ambitious, the district plans envisage three major museums anchoring an area completely devoted to heritage, culture and the arts.

Still to come in phase one is the **Guggenheim Abu Dhabi**, designed by Frank Gehry, which will showcase contemporary art with a focus on Middle Eastern artists, while the **Zayed National Museum** will tell the story of UAE founding father Sheikh Zayed Bin Sultan Al Nayhan within the context of the region's history. Architect Norman Foster has translated Sheikh Zayed's love of falconry to design an avant-garde structure with jutting steel-and-glass galleries inspired by flight and feathers. Each 'feather' will contain a gallery highlighting different historical and cultural aspects of the country.

The second phase will include the **Maritime Museum**, designed by Japanese architect Tadao Ando, which will explore the Emirati relationship with the sea, as well as the spaceship-like **Performing Arts Centre** designed by the late Zaha Hadid.

Don't hold your breath for any further museums to open in the next couple of years, though. Fraught with delays since the district's inception (the Louvre's completion date itself was put back twice before it finally opened in 2017), and attracting worldwide condemnation over treatment of workers on the site, the project has received as much bad press as good. Work on the Guggenheim was suspended in 2017 when supplier contracts were cancelled, and construction remained at a standstill in late 2018. Likewise, construction tenders for the Zayed National Museum hadn't even been awarded yet.

and film screenings. There are also occasional temporary art exhibitions. Check the website to see if anything interesting is happening before you troop all the way out here. Otherwise, the time to visit is during the **Abu Dhabi Art Fair** (www.abudhabiart.ae; Manarat Al Saadiyat; 3-day ticket Dhs55; ⌚Nov) for which it is the major venue. (☎02 657 5800; http://manaratalsaadiyat.ae; Cultural District; admission free; ⌚9am-8pm)

Eating

Saudi Kitchen

MIDDLE EASTERN $

7 MAP P92, A5

This snug little den near the Mina Fish Market is decked out with partitioned, cushioned floor seating (no shoes please). It's the perfect place to try traditional, falling-off-the-bone lamb or chicken from the heart of the Peninsula in dishes such as *mandi* (slow roasted and served with rice and chilli sauce) or *madfoon* (slow roasted with nuts and raisins over rice). (☎02 673 0673; Al Teelah St, Al Mina Port; mains Dhs30-70; ⌚noon-1am; P)

Dinner Cruises

The Corniche and skyline form a magical backdrop for a leisurely dinner aboard a traditional dhow. Based next to the fish market at the port, Al Dhafra runs two-hour dinner cruises with a fixed three-course Middle Eastern meal, including nonalcoholic beverages. Sit in air-conditioned comfort downstairs or alfresco on the *majlis*-style (reception room) upper deck.

Shakespeare & Co

INTERNATIONAL $

8 MAP P92, F3

For a lunch of stuffed *saj* (flatbread), sandwiches or salad, the wide veranda here, with its old fashioned, comfy wicker sofas and low tables, is a shady, casual spot. There's good coffee and juices too, as well as pastries, if you only want a quick bite. (☎02 644 5515; www.shakespeare-and-co.com; The Collection, Saadiyat Island, in front of St Regis Saadiyat Island Resort; mains Dhs21-89; ⌚7am-midnight; 📶🥄)

Museum Cafe

CAFE $$

9 MAP P92, C3

The perfect place to rest up after viewing the Louvre's globe-trotting collection, this contemporary, light-filled cafe, looking out to the sea, has a crowd-pleasing menu which dips its toes into Middle Eastern, Mediterranean and Asian cookery. Munch on a camel mini-burger slathered with harissa sauce, a wild mushroom risotto, or miso-glazed salmon with daikon. (☎056 689 0019; www.louvreabudhabi.ae; Louvre Abu Dhabi, Saadiyat Island; mains Dhs71-139; ⌚10am-8pm Sat, Sun, Tue & Wed, to 10pm Thu & Fri; 📶)

Al Mina Modern Cuisine & Restaurant

SEAFOOD $$

10 MAP P92, A5

Most visitors steam on past this glass-fronted restaurant in the hunt for its more famous neighbour, Al Dhafra. That's a pity because the ambience here, once you're inside, is every bit as authentic with lots of old photographs on the wall and the catch of the day (priced by kilo) delivered virtually from dhow to dinner plate. (02 673 3390; Al Mina; mains Dhs45-90; noon-midnight)

Al Dhafra Restaurant

MIDDLE EASTERN $$

11 MAP P92, A5

This aged, flamboyant gem, with fading decor, sports a sumptuous *majlis* (reception room) that has entertained princes and sheikhs over decades. The lunch buffet offers an opportunity to sample local dishes, including *machboos* (a casserole of meat or fish, rice and onions cooked in a spicy sauce) or choose your seafood (priced by kilo) with salad-bar selection for Dhs30. (02 673 2266; www.aldhafrauae.ae; Al Mina Port; buffet lunch/dinner from Dhs120/99, dinner cruise Dhs150; noon-5pm & 6.30-11.15pm;)

Sontaya

ASIAN $$$

12 MAP P92, E2

You can't beat the beachy atmosphere of this restaurant, surrounded by narrow water-feature canals and looking out towards the sand. The pan-Asian flavours, and twists on traditional dishes, are spot on, from its prawn and banana blossom salad to confit duck in a red curry laced with lychee and aubergine. Bonus points for an extensive, and varied, separate vegetarian menu. (02 498 8443; www.sontayaabudhabi.com; St Regis Saadiyat Island Resort, Saadiyat Island; mains Dhs70-340; noon-3pm & 6pm-midnight; P)

Beach House

MEDITERRANEAN $$$

13 MAP P92, F2

Open for breakfast on weekends and lunch and dinner otherwise, this restaurant, with its emphasis on sunny Mediterranean flavours (think slow-cooked brisket with olives and tzatziki, and seafood cassolette) has an enviable location fronting Saadiyat's coastal dunes. In the cooler months, go upstairs to the Beach House Rooftop (p98) for arguably Abu Dhabi's best sunset views. (02 407 1138; www.hyatt.com/en-US/hotel/united-arab-emirates/park-hyatt-abu-dhabi-hotel-and-villas/abuph/dining; Saadiyat Island, Park Hyatt Abu Dhabi; mains Dhs115-205; 12.30-11.30pm Sun-Thu, 9am-11pm Fri & Sat)

Koi

JAPANESE $$$

14 MAP P92, E3

We're here for the sushi and the starters rather than the mains, with lots of little flavoursome morsels to graze on. Order up a tuna tatare on wontons and a seaweed salad, scallops on a California roll and

Island Escape

A 12-minute boat ride from **Zaya Nurai Island Welcome Centre** (Map p92, H2; 02 506 6622; www.zayanuraiisland.com; Sheikh Khalifa Hwy, Saadiyat Island) on Saadiyat Island, idyllic **Nurai Island** (day pass Dhs480, Dhs420 redeemable on food & drink; 10am-11pm) is touted by the island's only tenant, Zaya Nurai Island Resort, as the Maldives of the Middle East. It's a postcard-perfect getaway with calm beaches and sun-toasted sands.

Day passes (book through the website) include boat transfers and beach and pool access. To use up the food and beverage minimum-spend portion of the day pass, have wood-fired pizza on the beach at **Smokin' Pineapple** (02 506 6274; Nurai Island; mains Dhs75-125; 10am-10pm;). Dinner guests (boats from 6.30pm onwards) have no day pass or minimum spend.

a couple of rainbow and eel and avocado sushi and you've got some seriously good eating to get on with. (02 678 3334; www.koirestaurant.ae; The Collection, Saadiyat Island, in front of St Regis Saadiyat Island Resort; sushi Dhs40-159, mains Dhs92-330;)

Turtle Bay Bar & Grill GRILL $$$

15 MAP P92, F2

Amid impeccable landscaping and a large staggered outdoor deck over the side of the pool, this is an undeniably beautiful spot by day or night. Downstairs, dine on surf and turf classics or head upstairs to the rooftop bar to catch cool breezes with beach views and cocktails. (02 607 0000; www.rotana.com; Saadiyat Rotana Resort Hotel & Villas, Saadiyat Island; mains Dhs105-270; noon-midnight, from 5pm approx May-Sep)

Drinking

Beach House Rooftop ROOFTOP BAR

Don't be deceived by the unassuming back staircase entrance to this rooftop bar in the Park Hyatt (see 13 Map p92, F2). Climb to the top, and you'll be dazzled by incredible turquoise waters and panoramic ocean vistas. Atmospheric music at just the right volume and low lighting set the tone, though it's Mother Nature's stunning sunsets and gentle sound of waves lapping that really steal the show. (02 407 1138; www.hyattrestaurants.com; Park Hyatt Abu Dhabi Hotel & Villas; 5pm-1am Mon-Sun)

De La Costa LOUNGE

With a beautiful vista, comfortable armchairs and sophisticated tipples (cocktails Dhs55 to Dhs65), this lounge at Saadiyat Beach Club (see 4 Map p92, H1) is a delightful place to watch the sun go down across the water. Cooler months see DJs spinning on weekends. (02 656 3572; www.saadiyatbeachclub.ae; Saadiyat Beach Club; 5pm-midnight)

Buddha-Bar Beach
LOUNGE

The famous Asian-themed chillax lounge from Paris has brought its normally temporary beach-bar concept to Abu Dhabi – the first location to receive a permanent branch. This wildly popular spot has made a name for itself by setting its signature Asian-Mediterranean mix to a soundtrack of stirring lounge music with a Buddha statue or two for good measure. (www.buddhabar.com; St Regis Saadiyat Island Resort, Saadiyat Island;)

Navona Restaurant & Coffeeshop
CAFE

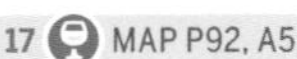

After a dusty morning slipping in and out of aisles of merchandise, haggling with stall-holders and photographing life along the harbour, you may fancy somewhere shady for a cold drink and a sandwich. Together with neighbouring Morka Restaurant, this unassuming cafe with both indoor and outdoor seating is a place to put your feet up for a while. (Area 5, Dhow Harbour, Al Mina; 9am-3am Sat-Thu, from 11am Fri)

Entertainment

NYUAD The Arts Center
ARTS CENTRE

18 MAP P92, G4

This multi-venue arts centre, inside the New York University's Abu Dhabi campus, hosts a regular, eclectic program of dance performances, music concerts, poetry open-mic events and film screenings. Tickets for events, usually announced a couple of weeks in advance, can be booked through the website. (www.nyuad-artscenter.org; East Plaza, NYU Abu Dhabi Campus)

Shopping

Fruit & Vegetable Market
MARKET

19 MAP P92, A4

This vast wholesale market, partly open-air, is the exchange point for melons from Jordan, potatoes from Turkey and onions from just about everywhere. A highlight is cruising along 'date alley', where shops sell around 45 varieties (from Dhs25 per kilogram). Giant *medjool* dates from Saudi Arabia cost Dhs70 to Dhs120 per kilogram, while medicinal *ajwa* dates fetch Dhs120 per kilogram. (Al Mina; 7am-midnight)

Walking Tour

Markets & Malls

Like many Gulf cities, Abu Dhabi has a penchant for malls. And for good reason. Collected under a roof, shaded against the heat and offering a single stop for most of life's necessities (eating, drinking, shopping and socialising), they provide a solution to life in extremis. This walk traces the origins of the mall in the city's early markets and ends in one of the capital's favourites.

Walking Facts

Start Al Mina; Al Mina bus stop

Finish Abu Dhabi Mall; Abu Dhabi bus stop

Length 5.8km; 2½ hours

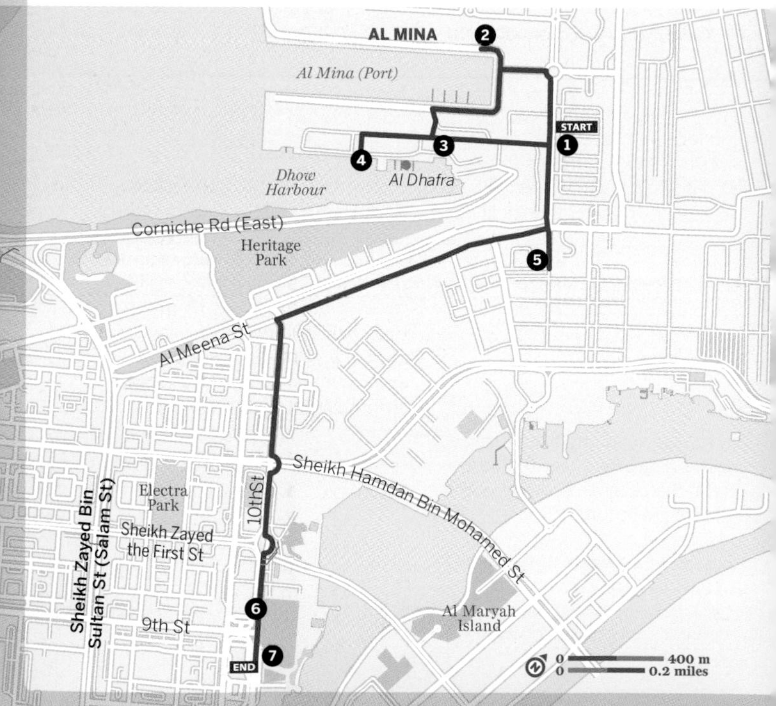

❶ Dates Alley

Everybody in the region will tell you the best dates are from their home town and then list the features of their favourite variety. Learn more about this life-supporting food at the **Fruit & Vegetable Market** (p99).

❷ Hardware Stores

Dates play an important part of the famous Arab coffee ritual and are served at social functions. A coffee pot and thumbnail cups make the perfect souvenir and can be bought from among the pots and pans of the **Iranian Souq** (p91)

❸ Fish Souq

You'll notice cacti for sale in the neighbouring nurseries, but contrary to expectations they don't grow in Gulf deserts. This is because in summer there's little difference between day and night temperatures. The water, too, remains uniformly warm, leading to an abundance of marine life – much of which is on sale at the **Fish Market** (p91).

❹ Dhow Harbour

You'll have seen lots of crustaceans being sold in the Fish Market. The Arabian Gulf is famous for lobsters and crayfish, which until recently were discarded by Emiratis in favour of tuna and sardines. You can see from the number of lobster pots by the **dhow harbour** (p94) that their value is now recognised!

❺ Carpet Souq

Dhows are handcrafted and adapted to the character of their skipper, but they invariably have one thing in common – an old rug thrown over the timbers and a handful of cushions. See where these workaday textiles are bought in the nearby **Carpet Souq** (p91).

❻ Khalifa Centre

For a much more refined version of carpets and *kilims*, stride out to the **Khalifa Centre** (p83) for a 30-minute walk. This 20th-century collection of independent shops bridges the gap between old market and modern mall and encompasses Oriental carpets and crafts from across the region.

❼ Abu Dhabi Mall

Wondering what's for sale from the Emirates in the Khalifa Centre? You're looking in the wrong place! The Gulf ports have for centuries been used as conduits for silks from India and spices from Africa. Hence the multinational flavour of the city's modern shopping emporiums, like the **Abu Dhabi Mall** (p83) opposite.

Take a Break

A great place for a break at lunchtime is Al Dhafra Restaurant (p97), a couple of blocks from the fish market, which offers an extensive and authentic Emirati buffet.

Explore

Sheikh Zayed Grand Mosque Area

The Sheikh Zayed Grand Mosque, designed by Yousef Abdelky, is not just an exceptional piece of architecture, it also represents the living soul of Abu Dhabi both as a place of worship and a memorial to the nation's founding father. The mosque is the key attraction but stick around if you're a foodie; there's fine-dining aplenty amid the resorts upon the Khor Al Maqta's shores.

The Short List

- ***Sheikh Zayed Grand Mosque (p104)*** *Soaking up the intricate detailing of this modern mosque.*
- ***Wahat Al Karama (p108)*** *Admiring the sunset mosque views from the plaza.*
- ***Li Jiang (p110)*** *Digging into some of the best Thai flavours in town.*
- ***Chameleon Terrace (p114)*** *Snaffling a prime spot for cocktail sipping with five-star views.*
- ***Souk Qaryat Al Beri (p115)*** *Checking out the boutiques, cafes and waterfront vistas.*

Getting There & Around

Bus 94 travels between the Louvre and the mosque. The Big Bus hop-on, hop-off tour bus stops right outside Sheikh Zayed Grand Mosque.

Taxis are the most convenient way of getting to the resorts either side of the khor (creek).

Sheikh Zayed Grand Mosque Area Map on p106

Sheikh Zayed Grand Mosque (p104) TORSTEN BAHR/500PX/GETTY IMAGES ©

Top Sight

Sheikh Zayed Grand Mosque

A masterpiece of modern mosque design, the Sheikh Zayed Grand Mosque is Abu Dhabi's iconic building. It's a triumphant vision that nods to the architecture of the Islamic empires and yet creates something purely singular. It's not just Abu Dhabi's most beautiful building but one of the most astonishing examples of modern religious architecture in the world.

MAP P106, D4

www.szgmc.ae

off Sheikh Rashid Bin Saeed St

9am-10pm Sat-Thu, 4.30-10pm Fri, tours 10am, 11am & 5pm Sun-Thu, 5pm & 7pm Fri, 10am, 11am, 2pm, 5pm & 7pm Sat

Marble Exterior

No expense was spared to construct the exterior, which cherry-picks design features from Fatimid, Mamluk and Ottoman mosques, as well as Indo-Islamic and Moorish architecture. The roofline, held aloft by more than 1000 pillars and punctuated by four 107m-high minarets, is graced with 82 domes all built from more than 90,000 tonnes of pure white marble. The vast central courtyard floor and columns are inlaid with a swooping cascade of floral mosaic design using lapis lazuli, agate, amethyst and mother-of-pearl, while the courtyard is rimmed by airy, columned arcades and reflective pools which cast a mirror image of the columns in their still blue water.

Contemporary Interior

The lavish interior of the main columned prayer hall is topped off by three chandeliers, which fill the space with shafts of primary-coloured light. The chandeliers, the largest of which weighs approximately 11 tonnes, sparkle with Swarovski crystals and shine with 40kg of 24-carat galvanised gold. Their highly modern design, along with the modern floral motifs inlaid with mother-of-pearl that swirl across the walls, give this vast space, which can accommodate 41,000 worshippers, a thoroughly contemporary atmosphere.

The Prayer Hall Carpet

The prayer hall's floor is covered by the world's largest hand-knotted carpet, covering 5700 sq metres in a traditional Islamic medallion design inspired by the design of court and palace Persian carpets. It's made from New Zealand wool and Iranian cotton, and 1200 artisans spent a year crafting the 2.268 billion knots it took to make.

★ Top Tips

- If you have time, visit more than once: during the day for the dome reflections cast upon the courtyard and again after dark when the lights come on.
- Dress in loose-fitting, ankle- and wrist-length clothing (with headscarf for women) to avoid donning one of the sweaty nylon, hooded *abayas* (a robe-like dress) handed out at the entrance.
- Head downstairs, at either end of the front arcades, to the toilets if you want to admire the marble ablution fountains (no photos allowed).
- The crowds are busiest between 9.30am and 3pm when most tour buses visit.
- Admission is free.

Take a Break

In the mosque gardens, Coffee Club (p110) offers up a full coffee menu, plus frappés and other iced drinks, as well as good sandwiches.

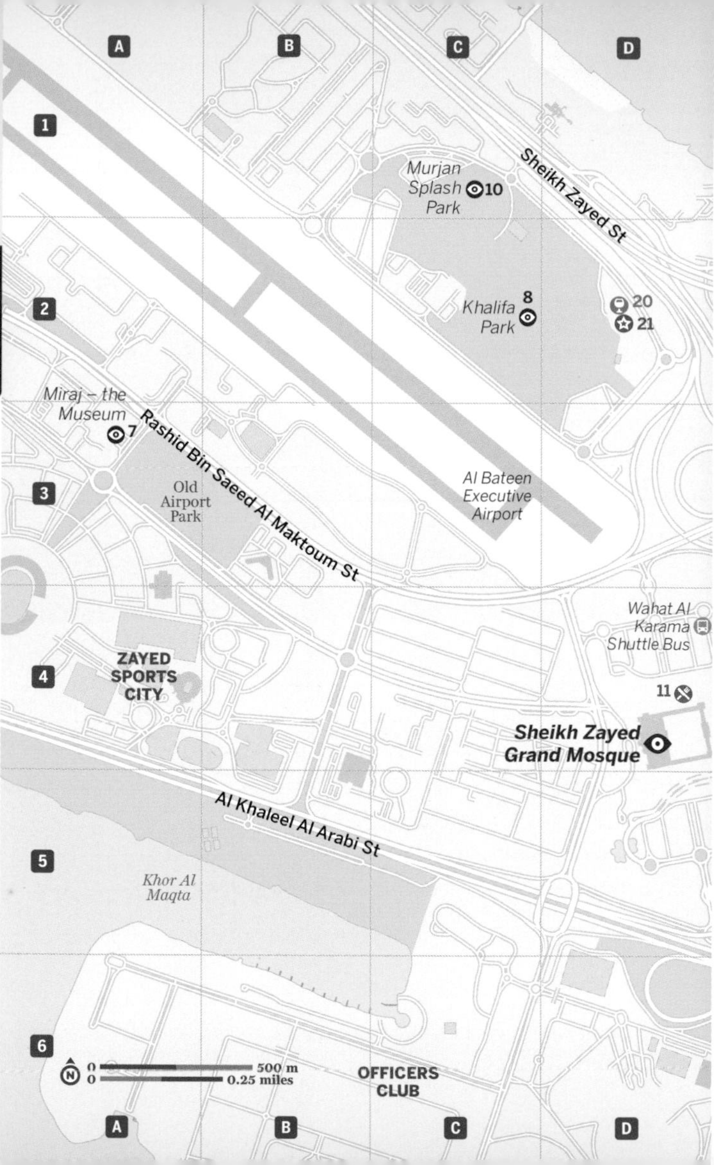

A B C D

1 2 3 4 5 6

Murjan Splash Park 10

Sheikh Zayed St

Khalifa Park 8

20
21

Miraj – the Museum 7

Rashid Bin Saeed Al Maktoum St

Old Airport Park

Al Bateen Executive Airport

Wahat Al Karama Shuttle Bus

11

ZAYED SPORTS CITY

Sheikh Zayed Grand Mosque

Al Khaleel Al Arabi St

Khor Al Maqta

0 500 m
0 0.25 miles

OFFICERS CLUB

A B C D

For reviews see

Top Sights	p104
Sights	p108
Eating	p110
Drinking	p114
Entertainment	p114
Shopping	p115

Sights

Wahat Al Karama MEMORIAL

1 MAP P106, E4

This memorial, opposite the eastern side of the Grand Mosque (p104), was inaugurated in 2016 in memory of Emiratis who have given their lives in service to the nation. The main monument, a leaning stack of 31 mammoth aluminium-clad tablets inscribed with poems and quotations from prominent UAE figureheads, sits in front of a Memorial Plaza fashioned from Turkish travertine stone built around a shallow, circular pool which reflects both the panels and the Grand Mosque just across the busy highway. (www.wahatalkarama.ae; 3rd St, Khor Al Maqta; admission free; 9am-10pm, tours 11am & 5pm)

Fairmont Bab Al Bahr Beach BEACH

2 MAP P106, G4

A day spent beach-side at the **Fairmont** (02 654 3000; www.fairmont.com; Khor Al Maqta; r from Dhs1154; P) is sandy relaxation, with the best views across the *khor* (creek) to the Sheikh Zayed Grand Mosque to boot. There's a separate children's pool area as well as a lap pool, and kayaks and SUP-boards can be rented on the beach. (02 654 3333; www.fairmont.com; Khor Al Maqta, Fairmont Bab Al Bahr; adult/couple/family/child Sun-Thu Dhs160/210/310/50, Fri & Sat Dhs210/360/410/100; 6am-8pm)

Shangri La Hotel Beach BEACH

3 MAP P106, G6

The Shangri La Hotel's palm-tree-dappled pool area and sweep of white sand out front is open for non-guest day access. There's a great poolside restaurant and bar for snacks and drinks while you sunbathe and swim. (02 509 8516; www.shangri-la.com; Khor Al Maqta, Shangri La Hotel; adult/family/child Sun-Thu Dhs200/400/100, Fri & Sat Dhs300/600/200; 9am-11.30pm)

Khor Al Maqta WATERFRONT

4 MAP P106, G4

This historic waterway separates Abu Dhabi from the mainland, guarded by the now somewhat hidden Al Maqta Fort and a small watchtower, on a rocky promontory in the middle of the *khor*. The mainland bank is home to a cluster of luxury resort-hotels and the Souk Qaryat Al Beri (p115) mall, all with restaurants and bars that have outdoor terraces with views of the snowy-white Sheikh Zayed Grand Mosque (p104) across the water. (Bain Al Jessrain)

Sheikh Zayed Bridge BRIDGE

5 MAP P106, F2

Said to symbolise the flow of energy into the capital, this 842m-long modern bridge designed by the late Zaha Hadid is one of three gateways to Abu Dhabi. Its curvilinear form is reminiscent of sand dunes, and at night the lighting scheme gives a sense that the dunes are on the move.

Al Maqta Fort & Watchtower FORT

6 MAP P106, G3

Despite being one of the oldest sights in Abu Dhabi, this 200-year-old guardian of the city was restored and then more or less abandoned after the visitors centre here closed (though word has it that a new, as-yet-undisclosed project is in the works). For now, although neglected, this old relic, with its companion watchtower on a rocky island in Khor Al Maqta (the so-called Abu Dhabi Grand Canal), is worth an up-close view – if you can find it! (Al Maqta Bridge; admission free, interior closed; 24hr)

Miraj – the Museum GALLERY

7 MAP P106, A3

Showcasing beautiful objects from around the Islamic world, including Persian carpets, calligraphy, ceramics and textiles, this private gallery shop–cum-museum is open for viewing. There's a lot to love throughout the labyrinthine galleries if you have the patience to tolerate the incessant lollygagging of the shop minders behind you – 'house rules'. (02 449 1041; www.mirajabudhabi.com; Sheikh Rashid Bin Saeed St; admission free; 9.30am-6pm)

Khalifa Park PARK

8 MAP P106, C2

This large and leafy park, not far from the Sheikh Zayed Grand Mosque (p104), has a number of

Wahat Al Karama

Friday Brunch Extravaganza

At **Giornotte** (Map p106, F4; 02 818 8282; www.ritzcarlton.com/en/hotels/uae/abu-dhabi/dining/giornotte; Khor Al Maqta, Ritz-Carlton Grand Canal; Fri brunch with/without drinks Dhs395/295; 1-4pm Fri), live dance shows provide the entertainment for one of the city's best Friday brunches. If that isn't enough sparkle for you, there are 27 live cheffing stations with the action including Wagyu beef carving and oyster-openings plus a globe-trotting buffet to suit all tastes, not to mention trips to a dedicated dessert room.

attractions, including a football playing area, fountains, ponds and waterfalls, lots of shaded seating, a children's amusement park and a small train that trundles around the site. (www.adm.gov.ae; Al Salam St; adult/child Dhs1/free; 3-10pm Sun-Thu, to 11pm Fri & Sat)

ESpa SPA

9 MAP P106, G5

With Marrakesh riad styling, a full re-creation of a traditional hammam (Turkish bath) and a tranquil outdoor terrace for relaxation, this spa is a soothing, tranquil and beautiful space to have your aches massaged away or to treat yourself to the full steam-soak-scrub hammam experience. (www.ritzcarlton.com; Venetian Village, Ritz Carlton Abu Dhabi Grand Canal; hammams from Dhs730, 1hr massage from Dhs590; 11am-8pm)

Murjan Splash Park WATER PARK

10 MAP P106, C1

Offers a range of water-based children's activities including bumper boats, a 'lazy river ride' and a couple of small water slides. Good for tots though older kids won't be too impressed. There's also a 'surf wrangler' for learning surfing with an instructor present. (050 878 1009; www.murjansplashpark.weebly.com; Al Salam St, Khalifa Park; over/under 1m Dhs50/free; 10am-7pm)

Eating

Coffee Club CAFE $

11 MAP P106, D4

If you need to put your feet up after visiting the Grand Mosque (p104), this busy cafe inside the complex is the perfect pit-stop, serving up brunch and lunch plates of French toast, omelettes and sandwiches as well as frappes, iced coffees and hot drinks.The toilets here are nicer than the ones in the mosque, too. (www.thecoffeeclubme.com; northern entrance, Sheikh Zayed Grand Mosque complex; mains Dhs32-43; 7.30am-10pm Sat-Thu, from 12.30pm Fri;)

Li Jiang ASIAN $$

12 MAP P106, F4

Asia's multi-layered, spice-tinged flavours are presented amid a red-toned dining room replete with gorgeous Thai textile detailing. Malaysian, Thai and Chinese flavours dominate the menu. Graze on crispy taro cakes, chicken satay and dim sum, sup up a spicy laksa or dig into mains of ginger lotus sea bass or massaman curry. Head here Monday for unlimited dim sum night. (02 818 8282; www.ritzcarlton.com; Khor Al Maqta, Ritz-Carlton Abu Dhabi Grand Canal; mains Dhs60-260; 6pm-midnight)

Ushna INDIAN $$

13 MAP P106, G5

Romantic and elegant, this place hums with appreciation for the complex cuisine of India, brought to the United Arab Emirates by a large expat community. There are many curry houses across town, but this restaurant offers some of the most luscious variations, alongside beautiful views across the canal to the Grand Mosque (p104), with a sustainable seafood commitment to boot. (02 558 1769; Khor Al Maqta, ground fl, Souk Qaryat Al Beri; mains Dhs56-201; 12.30-11.30pm;)

Milas EMIRATI $$

14 MAP P106, G5

Dark wood and neon announce that this is an Emirati restaurant for the 21st century. Classic Emirati plates of *machboos* (a casserole of meat or fish, rice and onions cooked in a spicy sauce) and *deyay shiwa* (chicken marinated in saffron yoghurt) are given contemporary makeovers while there are also lighter bites such as falafel sandwiches and European dishes with Gulf twists. (02 558 0425; www.milas.cc; Khor Al Maqta, level 1, Souk Qaryat Al Beri; mains Dhs29-99; 9am-11.30pm;)

Mijana MIDDLE EASTERN $$$

High-class Levantine dining in Khor Al Maqt (see 12 Map p106, F4) with tweaks on classics of the cuisine, five varieties of hummus and – rejoice fellow *kibbeh* fans – 10 varieties of *kibbeh* (meat-filled, cracked-wheat croquettes) to choose from. Leave space for *umm ali* (dessert of filo pastry, butter, raisins and nuts baked in milk) and shisha on the terrace afterwards. (02 818 8282; www.ritzcarlton.com; Khor Al Maqta, Ritz-Carlton Abu Dhabi

Traditional Emirati Feasting

The faux 'Emirati house' set-up and fake camel plonked outside the front door of **Al Fanar** (Map p106, F5; 02 448 1144; Venetian Village, Ritz-Carlton Abu Dhabi Crand Canal; mains Dhs52-83; 8.30am-10pm;) may get your tour-group radar buzzing but this place is actually a favoured haunt of Emirati families and regional tourists who come here for traditional mutton, seafood and chicken stews, *jasheed* (minced baby shark with onions and spices) and grilled seafood spiced with tamarind and date-syrup.

Grand Canal; mezze Dhs39-60, mains Dhs90-205; ⌚4pm-1am Tue-Sun; 📶🍸)

Punjab Grill NORTH INDIAN $$$

15 MAP P106, F5

The rich dishes of the Punjab are re-created here with views out onto the blue waters of the *khor*. Get your tandoor (clay-oven) fix with *chaamp taajdar* (Punjab-style lamb chops) or, for those who prefer mellow spicing, a comforting butter chicken. (☎02 449 9839; www.venetianvillage.ae; Venetian Village, Khor Al Maqta, Ritz-Carlton Abu Dhabi Grand Canal; mains Dhs87-271; ⌚12.30pm-midnight; 📶)

Barfly by Buddha Bar ASIAN $$$

16 MAP P106, F5

With a beautiful waterfront setting, Barfly is a self-proclaimed supper club with a Far East–inspired menu, where dishes range from wok-seared sweet and sour prawns and Thai chilli chicken to international classics such as herb-crusted lamb chops and risotto. The sushi and sashimi really steal the show though. (☎056 177 7557; www.barfly.ae; Venetian Village, Ritz Carlton Abu Dhabi Grand Canal; mains Dhs70-280; ⌚6pm-2am Sat-Thu, from 1pm Fri; 📶🍸)

Sho Cho JAPANESE $$$

17 MAP P106, G5

Stylish Japanese dining with delicious, if a tad minimalist, dishes. Don't miss the seared sesame yellow-tail starter or the delicate and decorative *maki* sushi rolls. Come in a group so you can order the sushi platters. There's a DJ at weekends. Reservations are essential. (☎02 558 1117; www.sho-cho.com; Khor Al Maqta, Souk Qaryat Al Beri; mains Dhs61-145, sushi & sashimi Dhs28-199; ⌚noon-3am Sun-Thu; 📶)

Bord Eau FRENCH $$$

18 MAP P106, G6

Bord Eau at the Shangri-La Hotel is *le* restaurant for French fine dining in Abu Dhabi. The classic French fare (onion soup, foie gras, chateaubriand steak) is flawlessly executed with a modern twist and the flavours are calibrated to perfection. With simple elegance (including reproduction Degas ballerinas gracing the walls), the ambience matches the refined quality of the food. (☎02 509 8511; www.shangri-la.com; Khor Al Maqta, Shangri-La Hotel; mains Dhs105-265, 5-course degustation menu Dhs450, 3-course set menu Dhs280; ⌚6.30-11.30pm; 📶)

Marco Pierre White Steakhouse & Grill STEAK $$$

19 MAP P106, G4

Carnivores only apply. A dramatic 'flame wall' gives the dining room a Dante-esque quality at this swanky pad, created by British celebrity chef Marco Pierre White. The menu focuses on quality cuts (such as wagyu and masterkobe steaks) prepared in classic English and Continental styles. (☎02 654 3333; www.fairmont.com; Khor Al

The Religion of Islam

One of the most memorable sensations of a visit to Abu Dhabi, especially for visitors new to the Arab world, is likely to be the haunting sound at dawn and dusk of the call to prayer. Although the chants of the *muezzin* (mosque official who calls the faithful to prayer) echo around the city five times a day, it's at sunrise and sunset that the 'music' of the mosque is at its most affecting.

Islam in the UAE

Muslims account for around 96% of the UAE's population. Unlike in countries where the sacred and the secular are rigorously separated, in the Arabian Peninsula religion informs all aspects of life, including culture, society and law. Recognising the integrity of religion and life makes sense of certain customs a visitor to the capital city may encounter, and in turn helps guide appropriate conduct.

The Five Pillars of Islam

There are five articles of faith that must be upheld by Muslims:

Shahada Muslims must proclaim the following: 'There is no God but Allah and Mohammed is his Prophet'.

Salat Five times a day (at sunrise, noon, mid-afternoon, sunset and at night) Muslims must pray – in a mosque if possible, but on a prayer mat by the roadside will do.

Zakat This is the duty of alms giving. Muslims are expected to give a portion of their salary to those in need.

Ramadan It was during the month of Ramadan that Mohammed received his first revelation in AD 610. Muslims mark this special event each year by fasting from sunrise until sunset through the holy month.

Hajj Every Muslim capable of doing so is expected to perform the hajj pilgrimage to Mecca, the holiest city in Islam, at least once in his or her lifetime. Muslims believe that the reward for performing hajj is forgiveness of all past sins.

The Quran

The Quran is understood to be the literal word of God, unlike the Bible or Torah, which Muslims believe were inspired by God but were recorded subject to human interpretation.

Transport Tips

- To hop between the Grand Mosque and Wahat Al Karama, there are free **shuttle buses** (Map p106, D4) every 30 minutes between 10am and 6pm daily. They leave from the mosque's north parking lot (car park D).
- Traditional wooden **abra** (Map p106, G5; 050 133 2060; www.captaintonys.ae; adult/child Dhs25/free; 4-10pm Sun-Thu, 10am-11pm Fri & Sat) boats ferry passengers around the Khor Al Maqta, stopping at Shangri-La Hotel, Ritz-Carlton Hotel, Fairmont Hotel and Souk Qaryat Al Beri, on a hop-on, hop-off basis. Pay on the boat. Kids under six go free.

Maqta, Fairmont Bab Al Bhar; steaks Dhs199-759; 6pm-midnight;)

Drinking

Chameleon Terrace BAR

In the cooler months, the ground floor of the Fairmont Bab Al Bahr (see 2 Map p106, G4) is the place to be. Cool cucumber mojitos, passion-fruit Collins, and kiwi gin and tonics are just some of the signature cocktails (Dhs55 to Dhs95) you can enjoy on this outdoor terrace, with Grand Mosque views in the distance. (02 654 3238; www.fairmont.com; Khor Al Maqta, Fairmont Bab Al Bahr; 6pm-1am Nov-Apr;)

Cooper's PUB

20 MAP P106, D2

A well-established pub, with an old-fashioned, wood-panelled, brass-trimmed ambience, this watering hole is renowned for its popular ladies nights (Monday to Friday, though Tuesday is limited to teachers and cabin crew) with complimentary spirits. The pub grub is good here too. The massive rectangular bar boasts 48 taps – including one UK craft lager (Frontier) – serving 12 different beers. (www.rotana.com; Salam St, Khalifa Park, Park Rotana Abu Dhabi; noon-2.30am Sun-Wed, to 3.30am Fri & Sat;)

Ess Lounge LOUNGE

The beachfront bar of the Shangri La Hotel (see 3 Map p106, G6) is a relaxed place to shrug off the big city and relax with a shisha while drinking a cocktail, mocktail or beer while watching the sun set over the Sheikh Zayed Grand Mosque. (Khor Al Maqta, Shangri La Hotel; 5pm-midnight)

Entertainment

Laughter Factory COMEDY

21 MAP P106, D2

Abu Dhabi's top venue for catching international comedy gigs, with big names on the comedy circuit regularly performing here. Check the website for upcoming events. (www.thelaughterfactory.com; Salam St, Khalifa Park, Park Rotana Abu Dhabi)

Shopping

Souk Qaryat Al Beri

MALL

22 MAP P106, G5

This small mall's 21st-century take on the classic souq gets a thumbs-up for its appealing Middle Eastern architecture and waterfront location. The shops here stock items with roots in Arabia including oil-based perfumes and chocolate-covered dates. There's also a couple of art stores which sell original, contemporary crafts a step above what you'll find in most gift-type shops in Abu Dhabi. (02 558 1670; www.soukqaryatalberi.com; Khor Al Maqta; 10am-10pm Sun-Wed, to 11pm Thu, 3-11pm Fri)

Gallery One

ART GALLERY

23 MAP P106, G5

A one-stop shop for quirky, fun and original gifts and artwork. Pick up colourful mugs and placemats stamped with Arabic phrases *Yallah!* (let's go!) or *Ma fi mushkila* (no problem), camel sculpture puzzles and tote bags printed with *khamsa* (hand of Fatima) designs. There's also a wide range of art prints, notebooks and stationery. (02 558 1822; www.g-1.com; Khor Al Maqta, ground fl, Souk Qaryat Al Beri; 10am-10pm Sun-Wed, to 11pm Thu, 3-11pm Fri)

Bateel Boutique

FOOD

Located in Souk Qaryat Al Beri (see 22 Map p106, G5) this is a foodie nirvana, elevating the humble date to gourmet levels. Select a range of different varieties from the Medjool to the *khidri* or go straight for a decadent selection of these tiny fruits stuffed with fillings of candied ginger or smothered in chocolate. (www.bateel.com; Khor Al Maqta, 1st fl, Souk Qaryat Al Beri; 10am-10pm Sun-Wed, to 11pm Thu, 3-11pm Fri)

Al Saadah Art Gallery

CERAMICS

24 MAP P106, G5

These hand-painted ceramic tiles are an original and easy-to-pack memento of your trip. There are both traditional Islamic tile decorations and more modern takes on this art form to choose from as well as larger pieces – tables, stools etc – using tiles in their design. (Khor Al Maqta, 2nd fl, Souk Qaryat Al Beri; 10am-10pm Sun-Wed, to 11pm Thu, 3-11pm Fri)

Camel Cookies

FOOD

25 MAP P106, G5

Cookies with a local twist using flavours such as cardamom, pistachio, dates, saffron and Arabic coffee as ingredients. There's another branch in **Yas Mall** (www.camelcookies.com; ground fl; 10am-10pm Sat-Wed, to midnight Thu & Fri). Buy a pack of six to take the flavours of Abu Dhabi home with you. (www.camelcookies.com; Khor Al Maqta, 1st fl, Souk Qaryat Al Beri; 10am-10pm Sun-Wed, to 11pm Thu, 3-11pm Fri)

Explore Yas Island

Yas Island has blossomed into the capital's adrenaline hub. While the Grand Prix attracts a global audience in November, fun-seekers young and old visit year-round for the rides and simulations at Ferrari World, Warner Bros World and Waterworld. Away from the family-friendly thrills and spills, the mammoth Yas Mall has crowned the island as Abu Dhabi's premier shopping destination.

The Short List

- ***Abu Dhabi Grand Prix (p119)*** *Getting tickets for the city's premier event.*
- ***Ferrari World Abu Dhabi (p123)*** *Testing your thrill-seeker mettle on the roller coasters.*
- ***Yas Beach (p123)*** *Taking a relaxed approach to Yas Island by slothing on this stretch of sand.*
- ***Felini Garden (p124)*** *Brunching at this hotspot, where a lazy Friday of Italian flavours overlooking beach dunes beckons.*
- ***Yas Mall (p129)*** *Shopping an afternoon away amid this contemporary cocoon.*

Getting There & Around

The Yas Express free shuttle connects the main attractions of Yas Island with Saadiyat Island. Bus 180 connects Yas Mall and Ferrari World with Al Wahda bus station via downtown. Big Bus Abu Dhabi offers an audio-guided route around Yas, connecting with the main Big Bus route at Sheikh Zayed Mosque. It includes a visit to Masdar City.

Yas Island Map on p122

Yas Hotel (p145) at Yas Marina ELENA BEE/SHUTTERSTOCK ©

Top Sight

Yas Marina Circuit

Hallowed ground for Formula One fans, Yas Marina Circuit bursts into life each November during the Abu Dhabi Grand Prix. If you couldn't snag a ticket or landed in Abu Dhabi outside of racing time, there are still ways to get track-side at this iconic Formula One destination.

MAP P122, B3

02 659 9800

www.yasmarinacircuit.ae

off Yas Leisure Dr

2hr venue tours Dhs130

tours 10am & 2pm Tue-Sat

F1 Abu Dhabi Grand Prix

Each November the glamorous **Formula One** (☎02 659 9800; www.yasmarinacircuit.com; Yas Marina Circuit; 2-day ticket from Dhs1970; ⊙Nov) circus revs into action and a surge of international racing fans descends on Abu Dhabi. Held for the first time in 2009, this is the last race of the Formula One season. The three-day program includes Formula 2 and GP3 Series racing and after-race concerts by international artists; concert entry is included in the ticket price. It all culminates in the Formula One twilight race, showing off this spectacular circuit to its best advantage, especially as the race passes through the middle of Yas Hotel with its incredible mantle of lights. The total length of Yas Marina Circuit is 5.554km, and the 55 laps clocked up during the Formula One race results in a race length of 305.355 km.

Circuit Tours

Except during the Grand Prix, it's possible to tour the circuit, which is a great opportunity to see behind the scenes of one of the world's most glamorous car races. Tours stop at the North Grandstand, the Yas Marina, Shams Tower and the Yas Drag Racing strip and provides insight into the high-tech facilities needed to support an event of this magnitude.

Driving in the Fast Lane

Channel your inner Lewis Hamilton and be champion of the track yourself. Outside of the racing calendar, **DriveYas** (☎02 659 9800; www.yasmarinacircuit.com; Yas Marina Circuit; driver/passenger rides from Dhs690/350; ⊙9am-11pm) offers up the opportunity to get behind the wheel of a racing car on the famed Yas Marina Circuit or (if you don't fancy being in the driving seat) experience racing speed from the passenger seat. It's the closest you'll come to Formula One driving.

★ Top Tips

- Want to see the track but don't want to shell out for a tour? No worries. The gates are thrown open for free three evenings a week (6-10pm Tuesday, Wednesday & Sunday) for joggers, runners, walkers and cyclists. If you don't want to queue on entry, register on the Yas Marina Circuit website in advance.
- Bookings for all DriveYas circuit experiences need to be made a week in advance, so pre-planning is vital.

✕ Take a Break

For a lunchtime view of the grandstand's facade, a table on the terrace of Cipriani (p126) in the marina is perfect.

For late-evening cocktails with views directly looking down on the track, head to Empire Yas (p127).

Top Sight

Masdar City

Rising up at the centre of vast construction sites, the core hub of Masdar City sits like a sci-fi vision of future city planning. Built with serious environmental considerations, this experiment in eco-architecture was initially conceived as the world's first carbon-zero city, completely powered by renewable energy. Head here for a peek at the inspiration for future cities.

MAP P122, C6

800 627 327

www.masdar.ae

btwn Hwys E10 & E20

admission free

9am-5pm Sun-Thu

An Experiment in Sustainable Urban Development

Cities occupy around 2% of the world's landmass but demand 80% of the world's resources and are responsible for 75% of its carbon emissions. Masdar City is an experiment in sustainable urban development that looks at the possible ways to counter those figures. The city plan melds cutting-edge green technology with solutions from traditional Middle Eastern architecture design (narrow shaded streets, angled to catch breezes) to both harness the energy and protect from the sun. Hugely ambitious from the project's start in 2008, the initial carbon-neutral hopes haven't worked out, and with only the downtown portion of the project finished, the completion date has been pushed to 2030. For now, the weird ghost-town feel of this near empty 'city centre' exudes a sci-fi atmosphere. It's like being in a movie set when all the actors have left. As you wander, notice the 45m wind tower that channels cooler air to the courtyard below, solar panels on the Knowledge Centre and reflective building facades that minimise heat transfer.

Future Plans

When finished in 2030, Masdar City is expected to house 40,000 residents in a tailor-made green environment, and attract an additional 50,000 commuters. Detractors have noted that it's a neighbourhood built only for the rich and that its initial ideals have been diluted, while its cheerleaders say that despite the area failing in its initial dream to be zero carbon, Masdar City is an important step in the evolution of sustainable cities.

★ Top Tips

- Download the Masdar City Visitor's Map from the Masdar website before visiting, for information on the buildings and a plan of the site.
- A scale model of the site, once completed, can be seen downstairs in the Masdar Building.
- Ride (at 40km/h) on the electric-powered, driverless Personal Rapid Transit (PRT) system, which runs through some of the centre from the Masdar building.
- Sign a digital guest book for a unique, computer-generated legacy of your visit.

Take a Break

For seriously good coffee, a healthy smoothie or fresh juice, put your feet up at Skinny Genie (p128).

The globe-trotting menu at Jim's Kitchen Table (p126) has something to please everyone, from burgers to tacos and on to American-style pancakes.

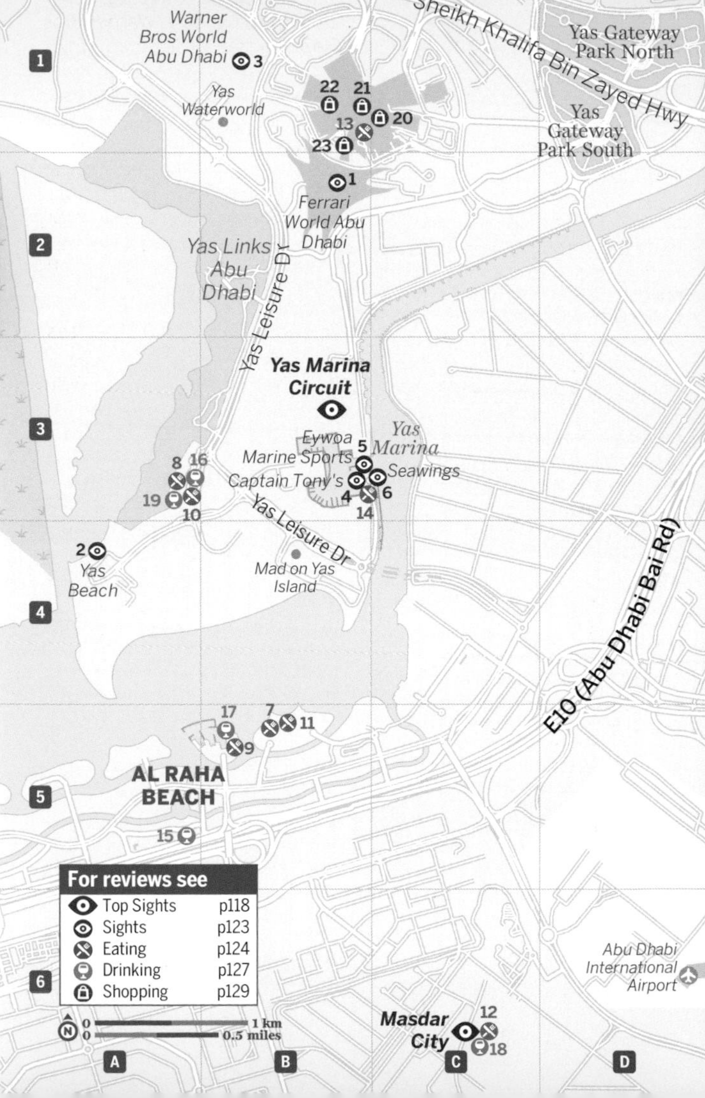
A
B
C
D
1
2
3
4
5
6
Sheikh Khalifa Bin Zayed Hwy
Yas Gateway Park North
Yas Gateway Park South
Warner Bros World Abu Dhabi
3
Yas Waterworld
22
21
13
20
23
1
Ferrari World Abu Dhabi
Yas Links Abu Dhabi
Yas Leisure Dr
Yas Marina Circuit
Yas Marina
Eywoa
5
Marine Sports
Captain Tony's
Seawings
4
6
14
8
16
19
10
2
Yas Beach
Mad on Yas Island
17
7
11
9
AL RAHA BEACH
15
E10 (Abu Dhabi Bai Rd)
Abu Dhabi International Airport
Masdar City
12
18
0
1 km
0
0.5 miles
N
For reviews see
Top Sights p118
Sights p123
Eating p124
Drinking p127
Shopping p129

Sights

Ferrari World Abu Dhabi AMUSEMENT PARK

1 MAP P122, B2

If you want bragging rights to having 'done' **Formula Rossa**, the world's fastest roller coaster, visit this indoor (perfect in summer) temple of torque and celebration of all things Ferrari in a spectacular building. Accelerating from 0km/h to 240km/h in 4.9 seconds, this is as close to an F1 experience as most of us are likely to get. (02 496 8000; www.ferrariworldabudhabi.com; Yas Leisure Dr; adult/child under 1.3m from Dhs295/230, with Yas Waterworld from Dhs395; 11am 8pm)

Yas Beach BEACH

2 MAP P122, A4

A surprisingly low-key corner of this high-tech island, Yas Beach is a lovely place to relax and enjoy the sea views, dabble in some water sports or generally chill with a cool beer. The kitchen rustles up grilled local fish and other tasty light bites. A DJ plays soothing sounds during Friday pool parties. (056 242 0435; www.yasbeach.ae; adult/child Sun-Thu Dhs60/free, Fri & Sat Dhs 120/free; 10am-sunset)

Warner Bros World Abu Dhabi AMUSEMENT PARK

3 MAP P122, B1

The world's first Warner Bros–branded theme park is a hit with kids and adults alike (DC Comics fans, we're talking to you). Spread among six 'Lands' – Warner Bros Plaza, Metropolis, Gotham City, Cartoon Junction, Bedrock and Dynamite Gulch – are 29 rides, entertaining shows and interactive attractions, all indoors and air-conditioned. (www.wbworldabudhabi.com; Yas Leisure Drive; adult/child under 1.1m Dhs295/230; 11am-8pm)

Captain Tony's CRUISE

4 MAP P122, B3

Offering a wide range of cruises with an ecofriendly approach, this company runs a relaxing and popular sunset tour, ecotours to the mangroves, and a four-hour escape to a natural sandbar with sandwiches, umbrellas, deckchairs, buckets and spades. Stand-up paddleboarding and fishing is also on offer. Most departures are from Yas Marina; prebook through the website. (02 650 7175; www.captaintonys.ae; Yas Marina; 90min daylight or

Theme Park Tips

Visiting the theme parks can be pricey, so a bit of pre-planning goes a long way. Simply buying tickets online in advance can lop 15% off the gate price, while if you're going to do the rounds, multi-park tickets further help your wallet. Keep your eyes peeled for promotions, which happen throughout the year.

Fun for the Kids

Yas Waterworld (Map p122, B1; ☎02 414 2000; www.yaswaterworld.com; Yas Leisure Dr; adult/child under 1.1m from Dhs250/210; ⏰10am-6pm Nov-Mar, to 7pm Apr, May, Sep & Oct, to 8pm Jun-Aug) offers opportunities to get soaked on 45 rides and slides as you follow Emirati cartoon character Dana on her quest for a magical pearl.

For little ones, **Fun Works** (☎02 565 1242; www.funworks.ae; Yas Mall, Yas Island West; wizz works/mini works Dhs60/30; ⏰10am-10pm Sat-Wed, to midnight Thu & Fri) has bouncy buildings, rides, rooms to reconstruct, play stations and toys. This interactive playspace is guaranteed to keep kids amused for hours.

sunset cruise adult/child Dhs250/150; ⏰8.30am-6pm)

Eywoa Marine Sports

WATER SPORTS

5 MAP P122, B3

Offering wakeboarding, wakesurfing, kitesurfing, SUP-boarding, kayaking and towed inflatables, this company has its finger on the pulse of the latest ideas trending on H_2O. (☎050 166 9396; www.eywoa.com; Yas Marina; 1hr SUP-board or kayak hire Dhs80; ⏰8am-6pm)

Seawings

SCENIC FLIGHTS

6 MAP P122, C3

If you like to make a bit of a splash on entry, then consider arriving in Yas Island by seaplane. The scenic tour takes 25 minutes and takes off from the sea at Yas Marina. Flights can take up to nine passengers. Book online. (☎04 807 0708; www.seawings.ae; Yas Marina; scenic tour per adult/child Dhs998/845)

Eating

Tawa Bakery

CAFE $

7 MAP P122, B5

Strictly gluten-free, this trendy bakery in the Al Muneer Beach development does breakfast all day (French toast, eggs Benedict, huevos rancheros), a host of pizzas, sandwiches and pastas and some decadent desserts (banoffee pie, pistachio eclairs). It's a hip spot – exposed air ducts and bake pans as decor and all – and you even get a beach view. (www.tawa.ae; Al Muneera Island Beach Plaza, Al Raha Beach; mains Dhs40-65; ⏰noon-10pm; 📶✍)

Felini Garden

ITALIAN $$

8 MAP P122, A3

This restaurant-bar with its terrace opening out onto the reed-covered coastal dunes is one of the most pumping places on Yas Island. Order up a pumpkin gnocchi or a prosciutto pizza and soak up the knockout indoor-outdoor setting.

It's renowned for its epic all-Italian Friday brunch (from Dhs170), which features a wandering saxophonist (jazzy!) and a sunset after-party. (☎02 656 2000; Golf Plaza, Radisson Blu Hotel; mains Dhs68-160; ⏰4.30pm-1am Sun-Wed, to 2am Thu, 12.30pm-2am Fri, to 1am Sat; 📶🍸)

Nolu's Café

CAFE **$$**

9 MAP P122, B5

California meets Afghanistan at this cafe charmer where almond butter and chia pancakes are offered alongside *borani banjon* (oven-baked aubergines with mint-flecked garlic yoghurt) and hearty fodder like lamb shank with brown rice pilau. The Afghan menu-spin comes from the secret recipes of the owner's Afghan mother. Wash it all down with fresh juices or an activated charcoal matcha latte. (☎02 557 9500; www.nolusrestaurants.com; Al Bandar Marina, Al Raha Beach; mains Dhs50-120; ⏰9am-11pm; 📶🍸)

Barouk

MIDDLE EASTERN **$$**

10 MAP P122, A3

Sit outside on the terrace at this good-value Middle Eastern restaurant for a casual evening meal of grilled *kofta saj* (meatballs in flatbread) or mezze dish selection of *fattoush* (salad of toasted bread, tomatoes, onions and mint leaves), vine leaves and falafel. There are more substantial main kebab dishes too. An after-dinner shisha (Dhs90) is de rigueur. (☎02 304 8108; Golf Plaza, Crowne Plaza Abu Dhabi Yas Island; mains Dhs30-150; ⏰6pm-1am; 📶🍸)

Ferrari World Abu Dhabi (p123)

Meylas

EMIRATI $$

11 MAP P122, B5

Whether you're here for a traditional breakfast of *chabab* (cardamom-spiced pancakes) stuffed with caramelised onions and cheese, or getting your fix of *machboos* (a casserole of meat or fish, rice and onions cooked in a spicy sauce) with a side of fried sweet potatoes and a ghaf leaf salad, Meylas is a great place to dive into Emirati flavours. (02 444 8884; Al Muneera Island Beach Plaza, Al Raha Beach; mains Dhs57-79; 9am-10.30pm)

Jim's Kitchen Table

INTERNATIONAL $$

12 MAP P122, C6

With an indoor play area reserved for little ones, this casual restaurant is a hit with families who come here for lazy breakfasts of berry and maple syrup pancakes or umpteen different omelette options and lunches of spicy fish tacos and pulled-beef burgers. There's vegetarian and gluten-free choices too. (02 491 9401; Masdar City; mains Dhs33-95; 8.30am-9pm;)

Cafe Bateel

MEDITERRANEAN $$

13 MAP P122, B1

Hailing from Saudi Arabia and best known for its exquisite date speciality shops, the cafe arm of Bateel is worth seeking out. Its largely organic Mediterranean-meets–Middle East menu with a healthy dollop of hipster (avocado and quinoa feature big) is good for salads, sandwiches and pasta. The to-die-for desserts include bateel date pudding with butterscotch and caramelised pecans. (www.bateel.com; Pavilion Cascade Walk, ground fl, Yas Mall; mains Dhs44-98; 9am-11pm Sun-Wed, to midnight Thu-Sat;)

Aquarium

SEAFOOD $$

14 MAP P122, B3

With extra-large aquariums gracing the interior of this casual-dining restaurant, there's no doubting its speciality. Outdoor terrace tables are coveted at night for views over the marina to the curvacious swoop of the Yas Hotel's roof. Either choose your fish and the way you'd like it cooked or pick a paella, pasta or sushi sharing platter from the globe-trotting menu. (02 565 0007; www.yasmarina.ae/aquarium; Yas Marina; mains Dhs75-149; noon-1am Sat-Wed, to 2am Thu & Fri;)

Cipriani

ITALIAN $$$

The menu may be a choice of Italian (including a lot of signature dishes from world-famous Harry's Bar in Venice) or Asian-fusion, but the view from this restaurant at the Marina (see **5** Map p122, B3) is distinctly Emirates. The terrace looks out over the grandstands of the Yas Marina Circuit (p118), designer yachts moored alongside, and the **Yas Hotel**, with its mantle of amethyst and diamond lights. (02 657 5400; www.cipriani.com; Yas Marina; mains Dhs111-400; 6pm-midnight)

Drinking

Stars 'N' Bars

SPORTS BAR

Voted Abu Dhabi's best sports bar, this wildly popular and rowdy bar and grill in Yas Marina (see 14 Map p122, B3) is unapologetically American. With 24 taps, including craft selections from Brewdog, Anchor Steam and Brooklyn Brewery, it's certainly a beer destination, but it draws hordes for food, live music and shisha too. Throw in nearly 80 TVs and there's something – and something on – for everyone. (02 565 0101; www.starsnbars.ae; Yas Marina; cocktails Dhs55-75; noon-3am;)

McGettigan's AUH

IRISH PUB

15 MAP P122, A5

This convivial pub plays all the big sport matches and holds a flurry of weekly events as well as regularly hosting local bands and singers. There's something happening pretty much every day of the week. Its relaxed, fun, casual scene – in direct contrast to much of the city's glitzy nightlife – is hugely popular. (02 652 4333; www.mcgettigans.com; Al Raha Beach, Al Raha Beach Hotel; 3pm-2am Sun-Wed, from noon Thu-Sat)

Belgian Café

PUB

16 MAP P122, A3

This second branch of the Belgian Café (p67), within the Radisson Blu Hotel, is a chilled-out spot for beer fans. Belgium's best brews are all available on tap or by bottle and major sports events are played on the screens. (02 656 2406; Golf Plaza, Radisson Blu Hotel; noon-2am Sat-Wed, to 3am Thu & Fri)

Pacifiko Tiki

BAR

17 MAP P122, B5

Ignore the tacky faux-Tiki totems on entry. In cooler months, the outdoor terrace of this curvy

Clubbing on Yas

Empire Yas (050 501 5052; www.capitalmotion.com; Bridge Gallery, Yas Hotel; 10pm-3.30am Mon-Fri;) occupies a bridge directly over Yas Island's Formula One track. It's flush with the city's party-hard, moneyed set of foreign residents. Monday (and usually Tuesday and Wednesday as well) is ladies night with free house beverages all night for women. Wednesday is RnB and hip-hop.

At **Mad on Yas Island** (Map p122, B4; 055 834 6262; www.madonyasisland.com; Leisure Dr, near Yas Tunnel; 11pm-3.30am Thu & Fri;), one of Abu Dhabi's see-and-be-seen party haunts, you can dress up and bring your ID (over 21s only) to hang with the beautiful people partying to RnB, hip-hop, house and grime.

timber bar-restaurant, jutting right out onto the water at the end of Al Bandar Marina, is made for sundowner cocktails (Dhs65 to Dhs75) or beers (Dhs35 to Dhs45). At happy hour (5pm to 7pm) slash 50% off those prices. The house band plays Latin tunes most nights. (☎02 556 6090; www.capitalmotion.com; Al Bandar Marina, Al Raha Beach; ⏰noon-2am Sat-Wed, to 3am Thu & Fri)

Skinny Genie — CAFE

18 MAP P122, C6

Healthy vegan-friendly cafe offering homemade almond milk, avocado smoothies and green vegetable juices along with *karak chai* (spicy tea) and a caboodle of espresso-based coffees. The shady and cool front patio, with exceptionally comfy seating, is a good place to put your feet up after exploring Masdar City (p120). Extra bonus points for the old-school soundtrack of '80s classics. (☎02 555 5897; Masdar City; ⏰9am-11pm Sat-Thu, from 11am Fri; 📶)

Iris — BAR

Late at night, this bar at Yas Marina (see 5 ◉ Map p122, B3) gets packed with trendy young things sipping signature cocktails (Dhs55 to Dhs75). DJs spin progressive deep house on Thursday and '80s classics on Sunday. From October to April the partying spills out onto the outdoor deck with the twinkling lights of the Yas Hotel across the water creating a suitably dramatic background. (☎055 160

Cipriani (p126)

LIZCOUGHLAN/SHUTTERSTOCK ©

5636; www.yasmarina.com; Yas Marina; 6pm-3am Wed-Sun;)

Stills Bar & Brasserie

BAR

19 MAP P122, A3

Based at the Crowne Plaza Yas Island and with live entertainment and the longest bar in Abu Dhabi, this is a happening spot for beer (17 taps), cocktails and a satisfying selection of upmarket pub grub, from burgers to fresh mussels. (02 656 3053; www.facebook.com/stillsbar; Golf Plaza, Crowne Plaza Abu Dhabi Yas Island; 3pm-2am Sun-Thu, from noon Fri & Sat;)

Shopping

FBMI

TEXTILES

20 MAP P122, C1

The beautiful handmade carpets on sale here are the backbone of Sheikha Fatima Bint Mohammed Bin Zayed's NGO, which aims to support and expand the economic opportunities of Afghan women; 70% of the weaving artisans it hires are women. All the textiles are made from wool and cotton sourced locally in Afghanistan and then dyed using traditional natural colours. (Fatima Bint Mohammed Bin Zayed Initiative; 02 566 9600; www.fbmi.ae; ground fl, Yas Mall; 10am-10pm Sat-Wed, to midnight Thu & Fri)

Yas Mall

MALL

21 MAP P122, B1

Bright, spacious and hosting 370 shops, Yas Mall is the star of Abu Dhabi's shopping scene. Look out for the growing plant wall and the two 12m-high tree-themed sculptures by acclaimed South African artist Marco Cianfanelli, with leaves inspired by Arabic calligraphy. There's access to Ferrari World (p123), cinemas, a fun park (p124) for wee ones and a Carrefour hypermarket. (www.yasmall.ae; Yas West; 10am-10pm Sat-Wed, to midnight Thu & Fri;)

Kashka

FASHION & ACCESSORIES

22 MAP P122, B1

Head here for a huge range of pretty, embroidered *jalabiyas* (traditional kaftans native to the Gulf) that make for wonderfully comfortable lazy weekend loungewear back home. (www.kashkha.com; ground fl, Yas Mall; 10am-10pm Sat-Wed, to midnight Thu & Fri)

I Love UAE

GIFTS & SOUVENIRS

23 MAP P122, B1

Pick up fridge magnets, key rings and easy gifts you can stuff in your wheelie bag – all emblazoned with the 'I heart UAE' logo – here. (ground fl, Yas Mall; 10am-10pm Sat-Wed, to midnight Thu & Fri)

Explore Eastern Mangroves & Al Mushrif

The middle portion of Abu Dhabi island is all about exploring Abu Dhabi's more natural side. Take to the water by kayak, SUP-board or boat in the Eastern Mangroves area to discover the coastal mangrove forests; while to the north, the manicured expanse of Umm Al Emarat Park is a lush, family friendly time-out from the city's glass and steel.

The Short List

- ***Mangrove National Park (p132)*** *Kayaking out on a tour through the tranquil mangroves.*
- ***Umm Al Emarat Park (p136)*** *Discovering just how fancy a city park can get in this mid-island oasis.*
- ***Abu Dhabi Pearl Journey (p136)*** *Learning about Abu Dhabi's pearling heritage while you sit back on the dhow deck.*
- ***Café Arabia (p137)*** *Breakfasting on Middle Eastern classics in this beloved community hub.*
- ***Home Bakery (p137)*** *Getting your sweet-tooth fix at the city's home of indulgent treats.*

Getting There & Around

Bus 170 has hourly services from downtown that pass by the Eastern Mangroves area. Nos 43 and 44 run south from downtown past Umm Al Emarat Park every 30 minutes.

Hail taxis off the street or phone to book a car in this area.

Eastern Mangroves & Al Mushrif Map on p134

Umm Al Emarat Park (p136)

Top Sight

Mangrove National Park

Abu Dhabi's swath of protected coastal mangrove forests are a nature escape right in the city. Come here to spot wildlife, delve into the fascinating ecology of mangroves or simply take a serene time-out. Once you're on the water here, with a backdrop of looming high-rises, the capital's full throttle hum melts away.

MAP P134, H2

www.ead.ae

main access off Eastern Mangroves Promenade

admission free

Mangrove Life

Covering 19 sq km, Abu Dhabi's Mangrove National Park is the largest mangrove forest in the UAE. Mangroves play a vital ecological role, protecting the coastline from tidal erosion, providing a haven for wildlife, and purifying the water. They are also highly efficient at carbon sequestration. Historically, in Abu Dhabi, mangroves provided a good source of building materials as the hard wood is resistant to rot and termites, which made it ideal for building boats and houses.

Touring the Mangroves

Although there's a good view of the dense lines of mangrove trees from the Eastern Mangroves Promenade, to properly experience the national park you'll need to take a tour. Kayak tours are particularly recommended as paddling allows access into the narrower channels between the mangroves so there are more opportunities for up-close encounters with wildlife. Tour operators offering kayak, stand-up paddleboard and boat tours have their stations at the marina on the Eastern Mangrove Promenade.

Spotting Wildlife

Mangroves provide a safe breeding ground for shrimp, turtles and some fish species and serve as habitats and nesting sites for migrating birds. More than 60 bird species either nest or regularly visit Mangrove National Park, with the western reef heron and greater flamingo (pictured left) the most prominent species to keep your eyes peeled for. Small critters which make their home in the mudflats such as the mottled crab can also be spotted by eagle-eyed visitors, while in the water you may be lucky enough to see turtles and even dolphins.

★ Top Tips

- Early risers reap the best rewards; you're more likely to see a range of this area's bird life and the many other critters that dwell here on an early morning mangrove tour.
- For keen bird spotters, the best months to visit are December to February and April to July.
- If you're kayaking or SUP-boarding, expect to get wet. Bring a dry-bag for your camera or phone, or leave the gadgets behind.

✕ Take a Break

For prime views across the promenade and the mangroves, head to the outdoor tables of Cafe Blanc (p138) for a thirst-quenching juice after your tour.

Make a beeline to Pepper Mill (p139) for hearty feasting on the cuisine of the subcontinent.

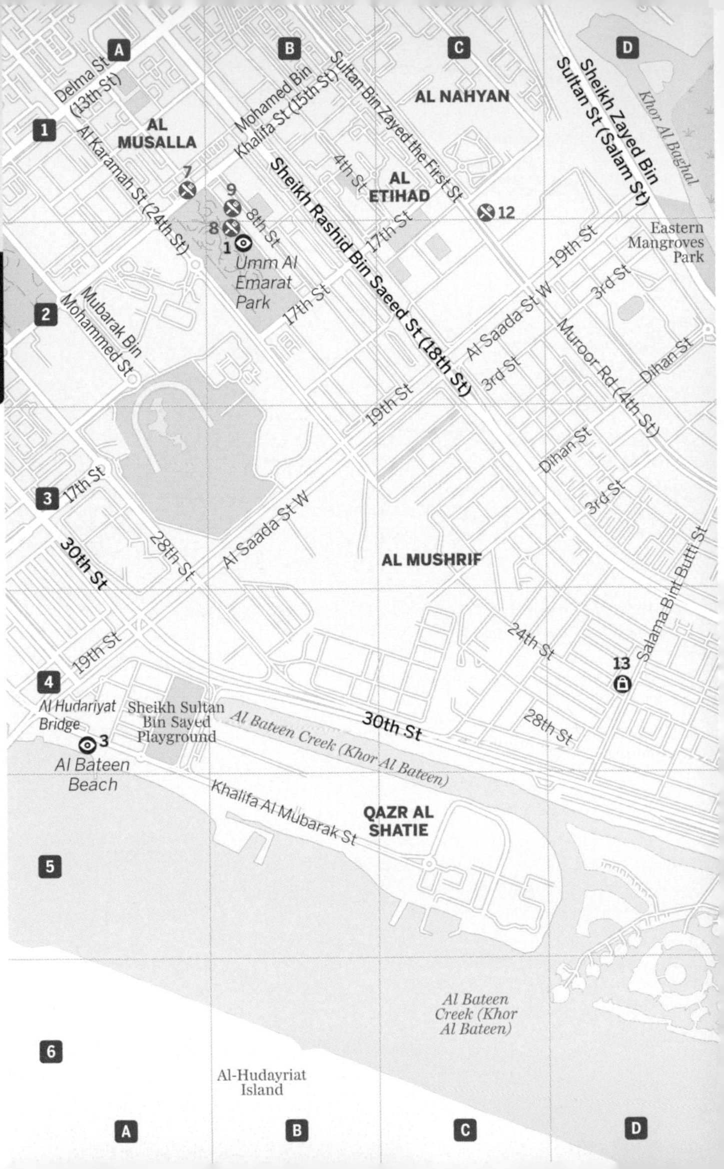

A B C D
1 2 3 4 5 6

AL MUSALLA
AL NAHYAN
AL ETIHAD
AL MUSHRIF
QAZR AL SHATIE

Delma St (13th St)
Al Karamah St (24th St)
Mohamed Bin Khalifa St (15th St)
Sultan Bin Zayed the First St
Sheikh Zayed Bin Sultan St (Salam St)
Sheikh Rashid Bin Saeed St (18th St)
Mubarak Bin Mohammed St
Al Saada St W
Muroor Rd (4th St)
Salama Bint Butti St
Khalifa Al Mubarak St
30th St
28th St
24th St
19th St
17th St
8th St
4th St
3rd St
Dihan St

Umm Al Emarat Park
Eastern Mangroves Park
Khor Al Baghal
Al Hudariyat Bridge
Sheikh Sultan Bin Sayed Playground
Al Bateen Beach
Al Bateen Creek (Khor Al Bateen)
Al-Hudayriat Island

1 3 7 8 9 12 13

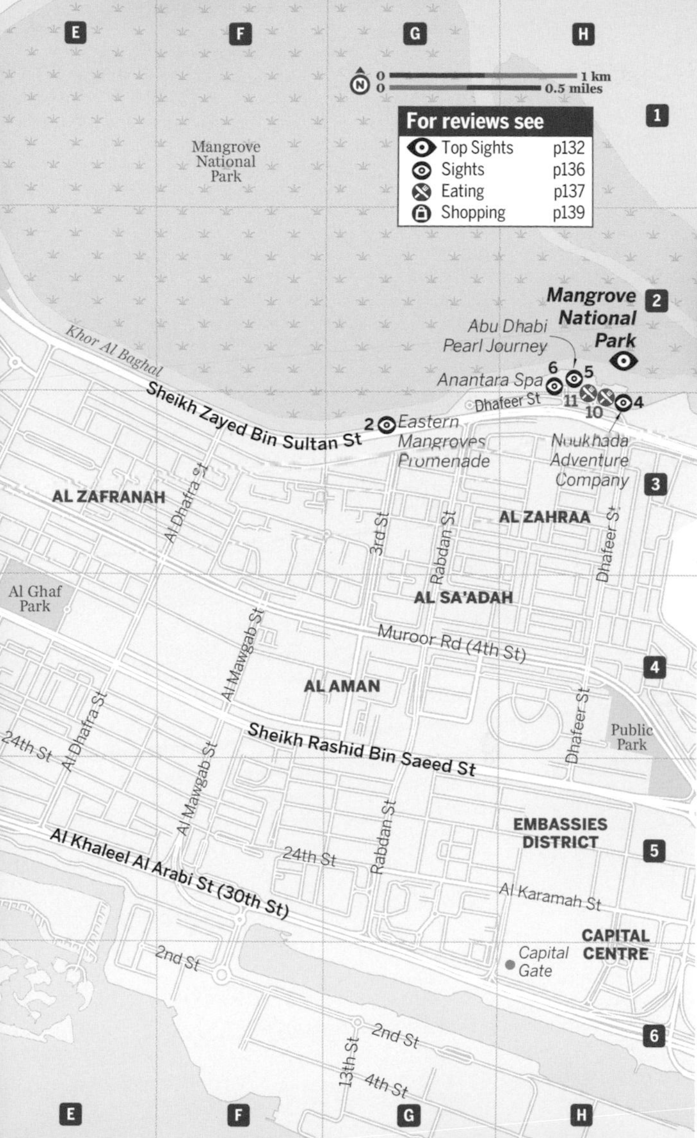
E
F
G
H
0 1 km
0 0.5 miles
For reviews see
Top Sights p132
Sights p136
Eating p137
Shopping p139
Mangrove National Park
Mangrove National Park
Abu Dhabi Pearl Journey
Anantara Spa
Khor Al Baghal
Sheikh Zayed Bin Sultan St
Dhafeer St
Eastern Mangroves Promenade
Noukhada Adventure Company
AL ZAFRANAH
Al Dhafra St
AL ZAHRAA
3rd St
Rabdan St
Dhafeer St
Al Ghaf Park
AL SA'ADAH
Al Mawgab St
Muroor Rd (4th St)
AL AMAN
Public Park
24th St
Al Dhafra St
Sheikh Rashid Bin Saeed St
Al Mawgab St
Rabdan St
EMBASSIES DISTRICT
Al Khaleel Al Arabi St (30th St)
24th St
Al Karamah St
CAPITAL CENTRE
Capital Gate
2nd St
2nd St
13th St
4th St
1
2
3
4
5
6

Sights

Umm Al Emarat Park PARK

1 MAP P134, B2

You almost walk away from this five-star urban park feeling like you've visited a museum. Manicured to perfection and full of design-forward and thoroughly interesting distractions, it more than justifies its admission fee. Highlights of the wonderful smoke-free space include a poignant memorial to the words of Sheikh Zayed; a three-floored shade-house with stupendous views; an animal barn with camels, goats, donkeys, llamas and the like for the kids to pet; a botanical garden, and an outdoor performing-arts venue. (Mushrif Central Park; www.ummalemaratpark.ae; 15th St; adult/child under 3yr Dhs5/free; 8am-midnight;)

Eastern Mangroves Promenade WATERFRONT

2 MAP P134, G3

The seaward side of Sheikh Zayed Bin Sultan St has been developed into a promenade to rival Abu Dhabi's original downtown Corniche, with a series of landscaped gardens, parking bays, picnic areas and paths. Offering excellent views of Eastern Lagoon Mangrove National Park, this is a good place to watch birds or dangle a line in the water. The eastern end, around the marina, has cafes and restaurants with outdoor terraces looking over the water plus several water-sports operators. (New Corniche; Sheikh Zayed Bin Sultan St (E10)

Al Bateen Beach BEACH

3 MAP P134, A4

A big wide strip of compacted sand, good for picnics and a spot of swimming and sunbathing. Umbrellas and loungers can be hired and if you feel like getting active, there are kayaks for rent. A couple of cafes provide cold drinks and snacks if you want to make a full day of it. (Khalifa Al Mubarak St, Al Bateen; admission free; 8am-midnight)

Noukhada Adventure Company KAYAKING

4 MAP P134, H3

Specialising in local exploration by paddle, this local tour operator runs kayaking trips through the mangrove forests, allowing you to experience Abu Dhabi's mangrove habitat up close. If you're interested in the ecology of this unique environment, opt for the two-hour eco-tour. There are also night tours and a monthly full-moon tour; both are great during the hotter summer months. (02 558 1889; www.noukhada.ae; Eastern Mangroves Promenade; 90min kayaking tour adult/child Dhs160/130, eco-tour Dhs220/170; office 8.30am-5.30pm)

Abu Dhabi Pearl Journey BOATING

5 MAP P134, H2

Ply the mangrove channels while laying back on the cushions

aboard this traditional wooden dhow. Cruises include presentations and information on Abu Dhabi's pearling culture past, plus Arabic coffee and dates. You're welcome to bring along picnic supplies to munch while you enjoy the scenery. The price is for the boat, not per person. No pre-booking necessary. (02 656 1000; www.adpearljourney.com; Eastern Mangroves Promenade; 1hr tour Dhs300; cruises 9am-7pm)

Anantara Spa SPA

6 MAP P134, H2

A celebration of marble, mirrors and water features, this spa is fit for royalty and offers up sumptuous and pampering treatments that merge tradition with modern methods. For baby-smooth skin the hammam (Turkish bath) rituals can't be beaten, while the massage menu is sure to revive jet-lagged limbs. (02 656 1146; www.abu-dhabi.anantara.com; Eastern Mangroves Promenade, Eastern Mangroves Hotel; 1hr signature massage Dhs630, hammams from Dhs525; 10am-11pm)

Eating

Café Arabia MIDDLE EASTERN $

7 MAP P134, A1

Housed in a three-floor villa, this cafe is run by a Lebanese arts enthusiast, Aida Mansour. Vast breakfast choices from avocado toast to *shakshuka* (poached eggs in a spicy tomato sauce)

More Lean than the Leaning Tower

Look out the window from many points in Abu Dhabi at night and you could be forgiven for thinking you've had one too many at the bar. Reaching skyward in the city's southeast is the 35-floor, dramatically tilting **Capital Gate** (Map p134, H6; 02 596 1234; www.capitalgate.ae; Al Khaleej Al Arabi St) skyscaper that holds the Guinness World Record as the world's most leaning tower – at 18 degrees westwards, it's over four times more wayward than the Leaning Tower of Pisa.

and a mains menu that waltzes from sweet potato and feta salad to *harira* (Moroccan lentil soup), falafel platters and a camel burger keep the crowds of regulars happy. (02 643 9699; www.facebook.com/cafearabia; Villa No 224/1, 15th St, Al Mushrif, opposite Umm Al Emarat Park entrance; mains Dhs25-90; 8am-11pm Mon-Thu, from 9am Fri-Sun; P)

Home Bakery CAFE $

8 MAP P134, B2

The United Arab Emirates is made up of a mere 10% Emiratis, and we'll be damned if you don't find nearly all of them sipping tea and savouring the decadent cakes at this trendy bakery-cafe inside Umm Al Emarat Park (p136). For something less sweet to eat there are gourmet breakfasts and sandwiches. (www.homebakery.ae; Umm Al Emarat Park, Al Mushrif; mains Dhs32-48; 8am-midnight; P)

Salt

FOOD TRUCK **$**

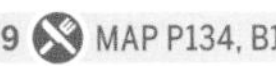

9 MAP P134, B1

Born in Dubai at the hands of a female Emirati-Saudi partnership, the Salt food truck had people chasing it all over the UAE before it permanently landed in the car park at Umm Al Emarat Park (p136), among other locations. The slick Airstream trailer does griddle-seared, grass-fed, hormone-free, halal beef sliders (two miniburgers) along with fries, ice cream and milkshakes. (www.find-salt.com; Umm Al Emarat Park; sliders Dhs32-53; 9am-2am; P)

Cafe Blanc

MIDDLE EASTERN **$$**

10 MAP P134, H3

We can think of few places more pleasant to sit in the early evening than the outdoor terrace here looking over the water while puffing on a shisha. Chuck a few mezze dishes into the equation – its house *moutabel* (purée of aubergine mixed with tahini, yogurt and olive oil) is delicious – and you have a perfect light dinner. (Eastern Mangroves Promenade; mezze Dhs28-45, mains Dhs68-75; 10.30am-11.30pm; P)

Salt food truck

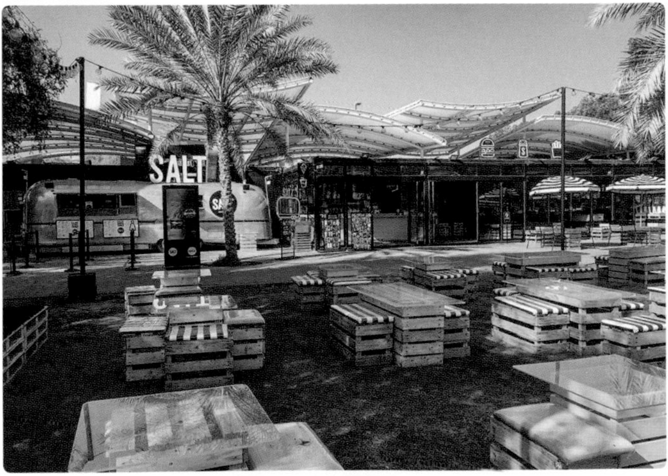

LINDSEY PARRY/LONELY PLANET ©

Pepper Mill

INDIAN **$$**

11 MAP P134, H3

Where you come to tuck in to rich classic curries and *tandoor* (clay-oven) dishes. The Pondicherry seafood curry of fish and shrimp is delicious. Top marks also for its creative vegetarian offerings, which go beyond the typical dhals, with *tandoor* choices of paneer cubes stuffed with mango pickle, and yogurt-marinated soy kebabs. (02 441 3582; www.peppermill.ae; Eastern Mangroves Promenade; mains Dhs38-84; noon-11.30pm; P)

Benjarong

THAI **$$$**

12 MAP P134, C1

This rather romantic, dimly lit restaurant furnished with comfy leather seating, ruby-red rugs and gold accents sits snug at the back of the Dusit Thani's ground floor. Order up *gaeng dang ped* (roast duck, pineapple and lychees in a red curry sauce) or a beef *phad king sod* (chilli and ginger wok-fried dish) to chow down on Thailand's flavours. (02 698 8888; www.dusit.com/dusitthani/abudhabi/dining/benjarong/; Sultan bin Zayed the First St, Dusit Thani Hotel; mains Dhs60-175; 7-11.30pm; P)

Henna Art

Before a wedding or party, Gulf ladies paint elaborate designs in henna on their hands and feet. The use of henna (made from the leaves of *Lawsonia inermis* mixed to a paste with essential oils) is centuries old and associated with sensuality. It takes three hours for the henna to dry and lasts for 10 days.

Shopping

Beautiful Henna Centre

BODY ART

13 MAP P134, D4

Henna application (on hands and feet) is a traditional ritual of local bridal preparation, though these days it's not limited to weddings and is appreciated as an art form in itself. With 20 years of experience, this henna bar offers both traditional and modern artistic henna applications in a luxurious salon setting. (02 634 3963; www.beautifulhennacentre.com; Villa 141, Salama bint Butti St, Al Mushrif; 9.30am-9pm Sat-Thu, from 10am Fri)

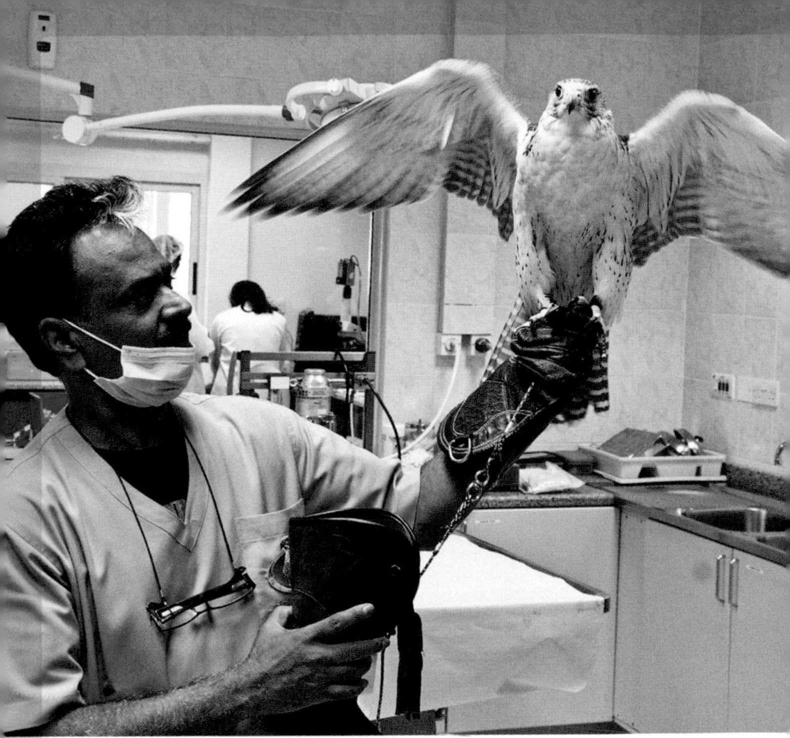

Worth a Trip

Abu Dhabi Falcon Hospital

This much-loved and -needed facility (the largest of its kind) offers a peep into the world of falconry: a thriving tradition that is an integral part of Emirati, and the wider Gulf, culture. No expense is spared in restoring these magnificent birds to full health, as a tour of this hospital shows.

02 575 5155

www.falconhospital.com

Sweihan Rd

2hr tour adult/child Dhs170/60

tours 2pm Sat, 10am & 2pm Sun-Thu

Origins of Falconry

Falconry is an ancient art that dates from at least the 7th century BC. The first falconer, according to Arabic tradition, was a violent king of Persia who was so entranced by the grace and beauty of a falcon taking a bird on the wing that he had it captured so he could learn from it. What he learnt, according to legend, changed him into a calm and wise ruler. Guided tours of the falcon hospital begin in the small **museum** by introducing you to the deep-rooted Bedouin heritage of falconry in the United Arab Emirates and its continuation as an elite sport today.

Meeting, Beak to Beak

The hospital here plays a vital role in keeping the birds (which can cost up to US$80,000) in top health. Guided tours include a visit to both the examination room where surgeries are carried out and the free-flight aviary where falcons can live while their moulting (the annual shedding and replacement of feathers) takes place. Watch close-up as the birds are prepared for medical examinations and the veterinarians carry out smaller procedures like feather repair and 'pedicures'. If you're willing to brave an arm, these well-behaved raptors will perch with you for the ultimate selfie.

Flight Training

It is no easy task to train birds of prey. Traditionally the Bedouin (falconers par excellence) netted their falcons (usually saker or peregrine) during their migrations, using pigeons as bait. On the tour you'll learn how they trained the birds through complex schedules of sleep deprivation and sparse feeding, retaining them for as long as it took to hunt fresh meat, and then set them free again at the onset of summer.

★ Top Tips

- Reservations (booked through the hospital's website) for the two-hour tours are mandatory and should be booked 48 hours in advance if possible.
- If you're travelling here by taxi, it takes around 40 minutes from downtown. Staff at the hospital are happy to order a taxi for you when the tour finishes.
- Don't miss the **Arabian Saluki Centre** (☎02 575 5330; www.arabiansaluki.ae; near Abu Dhabi Falcon Hospital; admission free; ⌚9am-1pm Sun-Thu), which you can visit for free in the same complex. A visit here involves meeting the affectionate and well-looked-after residents, picking up a puppy or two and perhaps watching bath time.

✕ Take a Break

Head to the Al Raha Beach area for a meal at Afghan-Californian fusion hotspot Nolu's Café (p125) or Meylas (p126) for Emirati dishes.

McDonald's

Survival Guide

Abu Dhabi International Airport (p145) MIKHAIL GNATKOVSKIY/SHUTTERSTOCK ©

Before You Go

Book Your Stay

- Five-star luxury hotels and beach resorts or business-trade-focused city hotels are what Abu Dhabi does.
- Whatever the budget, most are big multi-floor hotels. There aren't any boutique-style places here.
- Swimming pools are the norm, as are onsite bars, restaurants and gyms.
- Prices bounce around throughout the year, especially May to September.

Abu Dhabi

°C/°F Temp

40/104 – 30/86 – 20/68 – 10/50 – 0/32

Rainfall inches/mm

6/150 – 4/100 – 2/50 – 0

J F M A M J J A S O N D

When to Go

- **Winter (Dec–Feb)** Lashings of blue skies but chilly temperatures after dark and the odd shower.
- **Spring (Mar–Apr)** One of the best times to visit. Temperatures around 30°C.
- **Summer (May–Sep)** Avoid: temperatures average around 45°C with a stifling 95% humidity.
- **Autumn (Oct–Nov)** November's F1 Grand Prix is peak season. Hotel prices rocket.

Best Budget

Southern Sun Abu Dhabi (02 818 4888; www.tsogosun.com; Al Meena St; r from Dhs340; P) Swish styling, great staff; easily competes with hotels twice its price.

Novel Hotel (02 633 3555; www.novel-danathotels.com; Sheikh Hamdan Bin Mohammed St; r from Dhs420; P) Solid central city option with well-maintained rooms.

Al Manzel (02 406 7009; www.almanzel-hotelapartments.com; Sheikh Zayed the First St; studio/1-bedroom apt Dhs250/350; P) Well-kitted-out studios and apartments.

Best Midrange

Grand Hyatt Abu Dhabi (02 510 1234; www.hyatt.com; Corniche Rd (West); r from Dhs800; P) Sit on your balcony and soak up after-dark skyscraper views.

Rosewood Abu Dhabi (02 813 5592; www.rosewoodhotels.com; Al Maryah Island; r from

Hafilat Transport Cards

You need to purchase a Hafilat card (reloadable transport card, Dhs5 plus money for fares) before using any bus. These are available from vending machines at bus stops and at Al Wahda bus station. Hold up your Hafilat card to the validator upon boarding and exiting the bus.

Dhs600; P 📶 🏊) Sophisticated style and the best city dining and drinking at your fingertips.

Jumeirah at Etihad Towers (☎ 02 811 5555; www.jumeirah.com; Corniche Rd (West); r from Dhs847; P 📶 🏊) Landmark Corniche skyscraper filled with contemporary design.

Yas Hotel (☎ 02 656 0000; www.marriott.com; Yas Marina Circuit; r from Dhs750; P 📶 🏊) Minimalist rooms overlooking Yas Marina Circuit.

Courtyard by Marriott (☎ 02 698 2222; www.marriott.com; Sheikh Hamdan Bin Mohammed St, World Trade Center Mall; r from Dhs694; P 📶 🏊) Smooth service and comfortable rooms.

Grand Millennium Al Wahda Hotel (☎ 02 443 9999; www.millenniumhotels.com; Hazza bin Zayed the First St, Al Wahda; r from Dhs550; 📶 🏊) Business-trade-focused hotel with great staff.

Best Top End

Park Hyatt Abu Dhabi Hotel & Villas (☎ 02 407 1234; www.hyatt.com; r from Dhs1400; P 📶 🏊) Low-key luxury on Saadiyat Island.

Emirates Palace (☎ 02 690 9000; www.kempinski.com; Corniche Rd (West); r from Dhs1900; P 📶 🏊) Gold and glitz turned up to the highest level.

Ritz Carlton Abu Dhabi Grand Canal (☎ 02 818 8888; www.ritzcarlton.com; Khor Al Maqta; r from Dhs1470; P 📶 🏊) Full beach resort in easy reach of the city.

Four Seasons Abu Dhabi (☎ 02 333 2222; www.fourseasons.com/abudhabi; Al Maryah Island; r from Dhs900; P 📶 🏊) Art- and design-focused luxury.

Arriving in Abu Dhabi

Abu Dhabi International Airport

Abu Dhabi International Airport (☎ 02 505 5555; www.abudhabiairport.ae; Airport Rd), 30km east of the city centre, has three terminals including Etihad's base, Terminal 3.

Taxi

- Taxis cost Dhs75 to Dhs85 for the half-hour trip to the city centre, including flagfall of Dhs25.
- Only official airport taxis are allowed to pick up from the airport.
- Any Abu Dhabi taxi can dropoff.

Major Intercity Bus Services

Destination	Fare (Dhs)	Time (hr)	Frequency	Service
Al Ain	25	2½	every 30-45min	DOT bus X90
Dubai (Al Ghubaiba Station)	25	2	every 15min	RTA bus E100
Sharjah	30	3	every 30min	SRTA bus 117

Public Airport Bus

- Airport bus A1 picks up from arrivals area of Terminals 1, 2 and 3 every 40 minutes around the clock (one hour, Dhs4).
- It terminates at **City Terminal** (☎02 644 8434; www.abudhabiairport.ae; 10th St; check-in fee adult/child Dhs30/20; 🕑24hr, buses every 40min) in Al Zahiyah. To the airport, it takes the same route in reverse.
- To use the airport bus, purchase a Hafilat card (p144) from the vending machine at the airport terminal bus stop.

Al Wahda Bus Station

Al Wahda Bus Station (www.dot.abudhabi.ae; Rashid Bin Saeed Al Maktoum St) is 4km south of the Corniche.

- Buses within the emirate of Abu Dhabi are run by Abu Dhabi Department of Transportation (DOT; https://dot.abudhabi.ae/en/home).
- Buses from Dubai are run by Dubai Roads and Transport Authority (RTA; www.dubai-buses.com).
- Services from Sharjah are operated by Sharjah Roads and Transport Authority (SRTA; www.srta.gov.ae).

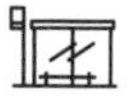

Getting Around

Taxi

- The government-monitored **Abu Dhabi Taxi** (☎600 535 353; www.itc.abudhabi.ae/en) runs metered taxis.
- Cabs can be flagged down or ordered through the call centre.
- Taxis charge Dhs5 at flagfall plus Dhs1.82

Road Names

Whether you're looking for Sheikh Zayed the First St, 7th St or Electra St will largely depend on what map you're using. The initiative to rename the city's roads from the former numbering system has resulted in confusion.

As former and current names are still common currency, here's a list of the main roads and their synonyms (without the street suffix).

Sheikh Rashid Bin Saeed Al Maktoom 2nd, Airport

Sultan Bin Zayed the First 4th, East, Muroor, New Airport

Fatima Bint Mubarak St 6th, Umm Al Nar, Bani Yas, Baniyas

Sheikh Zayed Bin Sultan 8th, Al Salam, East Coast, Eastern Ring, New Corniche

Khalifa Bin Zayed the First 3rd, Khalifa, Sheikh Khalifa Bin Zayed, Al Istiqalal

Sheikh Hamdan Bin Mohammed 5th, Hamdan, Al Nasr, Al Khubairah

Sheikh Zayed the First 7th, Electra

Al Falah 9th, Old Passport Rd

per kilometre. Between 10pm and 6am flagfall climbs to Dhs5.50. Dhs12 minimum fare is in effect at all times.

- If you have a UAE phone number you can book by downloading the Abu Dhabi Taxi app.
- Taxis are available for wheelchair users.
- Ride-hailing service Careem (www.careem.com) matches customers to private drivers. Cars are booked via the app. It operates like Uber (currently banned) but follows strict guidelines on ride pricing.

Public Bus

Abu Dhabi City Bus (www.dot.abudhabi.ae) operates 14 routes around the clock. Route map on website.

Most fares (see p144) are Dhs2 per ride within the city.

Useful bus lines include:

Bus 5 Marina Mall–Al Zahiyah–Al Maryah Island

Bus 54 Al Mina Fish Market–Al Zahiya–Sheikh Zayed Mosque

Bus 94 Sheikh Zayed Mosque–Al Wahda bus station–Al Zahiyah–Louvre Abu Dhabi

Bus 180 Al Wahda bus station–downtown–Yas Mall and Ferrari World

Tour Bus

For an informative introduction to the city, the hop-on hop-off service by **Big Bus** (Map p56; 02 449 0026; www.bigbustours.com; 24hr adult/child Dhs260/166; 9am-5pm) is hard to beat. The two routes, connecting at the Sheikh Zayed Mosque, pass by all major sights.

Tickets are sold online, on the bus and from kiosks near Big Bus stops.

Yas Island Shuttle Bus

The free Yas Express (www.yasisland.ae) shuttle bus links attractions at least hourly.

Blue Route Operates 9am to midnight; connects Yas Waterworld with the hotels at Yas Plaza, Yas Marina Circuit and Ferrari World.

Red Route Runs 9.30am to midnight between Yas Plaza, Yas Beach, Yas Marina and Yas Links golf course.

Essential Information

Accessible Travel

- Nearly all the sights, all malls and many other buildings have facilities such as ramps, lifts and toilets for wheelchair users.
- All midrange and top-end hotels have rooms fitted out for wheelchairs.
- Access to budget restaurants is more difficult.
- Pedestrian underpasses for crossing the main roads in the central city have ramps as well as stairs.
- The city's **taxi firm** (600 535 353; www.itc.abudhabi.ae/en) has specially fitted-out cars (which need to be ordered in advance) for wheelchair users.
- **Abu Dhabi International Airport** (02 505 5555; www.abudhabiairport.ae; Airport Rd) has a special check-in gate for travellers with accessibility issues and a meet-and-assist service called Marhaba.

Business Hours

The weekend is on Friday and Saturday. Many private businesses open on Saturday.

Banks 8am to 1pm (some until 3pm) Sunday to Thursday, 8am to noon Saturday

Restaurants noon to 3pm and 7.30pm to midnight

Shopping malls 10am to 10pm Sunday to Wednesday, 10am to midnight Thursday to Saturday

Souqs & markets 9am to 1pm and 4pm to 9pm Saturday to Thursday, 4pm to 9pm Friday

Discount Cards

- ISIC (international student) card-holders can get discounts at some restaurants and recreation services. See www.studentcard.ae for a full list.
- Etihad Airways passengers can access a bundle of discounts on theme park and beach entrance fees, spa services, restaurant meals and shopping purchases by showing their boarding pass at participating businesses. See www.etihad.com/before-you-fly/abu-dhabi-pass for full details of the offer.

Electricity

Type G
230V/50Hz

Emergencies

Ambulance	☎998
Police	☎999
Tourist Police	☎02 800 2626
Fire Department	☎997

LGBT+ Travellers

Homosexuality is illegal in the UAE. If accused, visitors can face deportation, fines or a jail term. Discretion is key.

- Unless you're staying at a five-star resort, where staff are likely to look the other way, it's advisable to book two single beds rather than a double bed.
- Most LGBT+ websites, including dating apps such as Grindr, are blocked.
- Despite this, because of the number of young foreign nationals working in Abu Dhabi, there is an active underground LGBT+ scene. Tapping into it can be difficult as a visitor on a short stay.

Medical Services

The standard of health care in Abu Dhabi is generally high, and emergency treatment is free. For locations of 24-hour pharmacies, call ☎777 929.

The vast **Sheikh Khalifa Medical City** (www.seha.ae; cnr Al Karama St & Hazza Bin Zayed the First St; ☎02 819 0000, ☎80 050) is one of numerous well-equipped hospitals in the city with 24-hour emergency service.

Money

ATMs are widely available. Credit cards are accepted in most hotels, restaurants and shops.

Islamic Holidays

Ramadan Month of fasting during daylight hours. Many restaurants close during the day. Most licensed premises stop serving alcohol. Tourist sites keep shorter hours.

Eid Al Fitr Three-day celebration marking end of Ramadan.

Eid Al Adha Three-to-four-day celebration commemorating Ibrahim's (Abraham's) sacrifice.

Islamic New Year Beginning of the Islamic calender's new year. Private businesses remain open.

Prophet's Birthday A national holiday.

Dates are approximate as confirmation is based on the sighting of the new moon.

HOLIDAY	2020	2021	2022	2023
Ramadan begins	24 Apr	13 Apr	3 Apr	23 Mar
Eid Al Fitr	24 May	13 May	3 May	24 Apr
Eid Al Adha	31 Jul	20 Jul	9 Jul	28 Jun
Islamic New Year	20 Aug	9 Aug	30 Jul	19 Jul
Prophet's Birthday	28 Oct	17 Oct	8 Oct	27 Sep

ATMs

- There is usually a charge (around 1.5% to 2%) on ATM cash withdrawals abroad.
- Some local bank ATMs charge withdrawal fees for cards not issued by their bank.

Public Holidays

New Year's Day 1 January

Commemoration Day 30 November

National Day 2 December

As well as set-date public holidays, there are several Islamic holidays with dates determined by the lunar calendar. Exact dates are announced in papers (www.thenational.ae) beforehand.

Safe Travel

Abu Dhabi is a very safe city to travel around during the day or night.

Drugs The UAE has zero tolerance towards illegal drugs.

Driving Keep a calm head if driving in the city. Turning without indicating and speeding into roundabouts are common. As a pedestrian, note that pedestrian crossings are a suggestion rather than a case of you having right-of-way.

Alcohol For tourists, drinking alcohol is only allowed in licensed premises. You cannot buy alcohol from a shop or drink in public parks, on beaches or on the street.

Dos & Don'ts

Clothing Modesty is key. Swimwear is only for the beach. Shoulders and knees covered at all times – for both sexes – is a good rule to stick to.

Greetings Men should refrain from shaking hands with a woman unless she offers her hand first.

Politics and religion Avoid contentious issues such as the UAE's involvement in Yemen and the Qatar blockade. Insulting Islam is against the law, as is publicly expressing sympathy towards Qatar.

Public displays of affection A no-no. Couples should refrain from kissing, cuddling or hand-holding in public. Technically all are public decency offences though most people turn a blind eye to hand-holding.

Ramadan Drinking, eating, smoking, loud music and dancing in public during daylight fasting hours are illegal.

Swearing Considered highly offensive. People have been prosecuted or deported for it.

Telephone Services

UAE country code	971
UAE access code	00
Abu Dhabi area code	02

Mobile Phones

- The UAE's mobile phone network uses the GSM 900 MHz and 1800 MHz standard.
- Mobile numbers begin with 050 or 055.
- Etisalat (www.etisalat.ae/en) and Du Mobile (www.du.ae) are the two main mobile phone operators. Both offer rechargeable pre-paid 'tourist plans'.
- 3G widely available, 4G increasingly so.

Internet-based Calls

- VoIP call services Skype, FaceTime and WhatsApp continue to be officially blocked. WhatsApp's texting function still works.

Tourist Information

Visit Abu Dhabi (www.visitabudhabi.ae) The city's main tourist-oriented website.

Yas Island Information (www.yasisland.ae) A good online overview of what's on, when and where on Yas Island.

Visas

- Citizens of 20 countries including Australia, Canada, China, Ireland, Japan, Malaysia, New Zealand, Singapore, South Korea, UK and USA can get a 30-day single-entry visa on arrival.
- Nationals of a further 40 countries, including nearly all European countries, receive a 90-day multiple-entry visa on arrival.

Language

MSA (Modern Standard Arabic) – the official lingua franca of the Arab world – and the everyday spoken version are quite different. The Arabic variety spoken in Dubai (and provided in this chapter) is known as Gulf Arabic.

Note that *gh* is a throaty sound (like the French 'r'), *r* is rolled, *dh* is pronounced as the 'th' in 'that', *th* as in 'thin', *ch* as in 'cheat' and *kh* as the 'ch' in the Scottish *loch*. The apostrophe (') indicates the glottal stop (like the pause in the middle of 'uh-oh'). Bearing these few points in mind and reading our pronunciation guides as if they were English, you'll be understood. The stressed syllables are indicated with italics. The markers (m) and (f) indicate masculine and feminine word forms respectively.

To enhance your trip with a phrasebook, visit lonelyplanet.com. For Lonely Planet iPhone phrasebooks, visit the Apple App store.

Basics

Hello.
اهلا و سهلا. *ah*·lan was *ah*·lan

Goodbye.
مع السلامة. ma' sa·*laa*·ma

Yes./No.
نعم./لا. *na*·'am/la

Please.
من فضلك. min *fad*·lak (m)
من فضلِك. min *fad*·lik (f)

Thank you.
شكران. *shuk*·ran

Excuse me.
اسمح لي. is·*mah* lee (m)
اسمحي لي. is·mah·*ee* lee (f)

Sorry.
مع الاسف. ma' al·*as*·af

Do you speak English?
تتكلم/تتكلمي انجليزية؟ tit·*kal*·am/tit·*ka*·la·mee in·glee·*zee*·ya (m/f)

I don't understand.
مو فاهم. moo *faa*·him

Eating & Drinking

I'd like (the) ..., please.
عطني/عطيني الـ ... من فضلك. *'a*·ti·nee/*'a*·*tee*·nee il ... min *fad*·lak (m/f)

bill	قائمة	*kaa*·'i·ma
drink list	قائمة المشروبات	*kaa*·'i·mat il·mash·roo·*baat*
menu	الطعام قائمة	*kaa*·'i·mat i·ta·*'aam*
that dish	الطبق هاذاك	i·*tab*·ak *haa*·dhaa·ka

What would you recommend?
اش تنصح؟ aash *tan*·sah (m)
اش تنصحي؟ aash *tan*·sa·hee (f)

Do you have vegetarian food?
مع ط كدن ع ؟ي تابن *'an*·dak *ta*·'am na·*baa*·tee

Shopping

I'm looking for ...
مدور على ... moo·*daw*·ir *'a*·la ... (m)
مدورة على ... moo·*daw*·i·ra *'a*·la ... (f)

Can I look at it?
ممكن اشوف؟ *mum*·kin a·*shoof*

How much is it?
بكم؟ bi·*kam*

That's too expensive.
غالي جدا. *ghaa*·lee *jid*·an

What's your lowest price?
اش السعر الاخر؟ aash i·*si'r* il·*aa*·khir

Do you have any others?
عندَك اخرين؟ *'and*·ak ukh·*reen* (m)
عندِك اخرين؟ *'and*·ik ukh·*reen* (f)

Emergencies

Help!
مساعد! moo·*saa*·'id (m)
مساعدة! moo·*saa*·'id·a (f)

Call a doctor!
تصل/تصلي ti·*sil*/ti·*si*·lee
على طبيب! *'a*·la ta·*beeb* (m/f)

Call the police!
تصل/تصلي ti·*sil*/ti·*si*·lee
على الشرطة! *'a*·la i·*shur*·ta (m/f)

I'm lost.
انا ضعت. *a*·na duht

I'm sick.
انا مريض. *a*·na ma·*reed* (m)
انا مريضة. *a*·na ma·*ree*·da (f)

Where are the toilets?
وين المرحاض؟ wayn il·mir·*haad*

Time & Numbers

What time is it?/At what time?
الساعة كم؟ i·*saa*·a' kam

It's/At (two) o'clock.
الساعة (ثنتين). i·*saa*·a' (thin·*tayn*)

yesterday ... ... البارح il·*baa*·rih ...

tomorrow ... ... باكر *baa*·chir ...

morning صباح sa·*baah*

afternoon بعد الظهر ba'd a·*thuhr*

evening مساء *mi*·saa

1	١	واحد	*waa*·hid
2	٢	اثنين	ith·*nayn*
3	٣	ثلاثة	*tha*·laa·*tha*
4	٤	اربع	ar·*ba'*
5	٥	خمسة	*kham*·sa
6	٦	ستة	*si*·ta
7	٧	سبعة	*sa*·ba'
8	٨	ثمانية	tha·*maan*·ya
9	٩	تسعة	*tis*·a'
10	١٠	عشرة	*'ash*·ar·a
100	١٠٠	مية	*mee*·ya
1000	١٠٠٠	الف	alf

Transport & Directions

Where's the ...?
من وين ...؟ min wayn ...

What's the address?
ما العنوان؟ ma il·'un·*waan*

Can you show me (on the map)?
لو سمحت law sa·*maht*
وريني wa·*ree*·nee
(علخريطة)؟ ('al·kha·*ree*·ta)

How far is it?
كم بعيد؟ kam ba·*'eed*

Please take me to (this address).
من فضلك خذني min *fad*·lak *khudh*·nee
(علعنوان هاذا). ('al·'un·*waan* *haa*·dha)

Please stop here.
لو سمحت law sa·*maht*
وقف هنا. *wa*·gif *hi*·na

What time's the bus?
الساعة كم a·*saa*·a' kam
الباص؟ il·*baas*

What station/stop is this?
ما هي maa *hee*·ya
المحطة هاذي؟ il·ma·*ha*·ta *haa*·dhee

Behind the Scenes

Send Us Your Feedback

We love to hear from travellers – your comments help make our books better. We read every word, and we guarantee that your feedback goes straight to the authors. Visit **lonelyplanet.com/contact** to submit your updates and suggestions.

Note: We may edit, reproduce and incorporate your comments in Lonely Planet products such as guidebooks, websites and digital products, so let us know if you don't want your comments reproduced or your name acknowledged. For a copy of our privacy policy visit lonelyplanet.com/privacy.

Jessica's Thanks

Huge thanks to everyone along the way who shared tips, advice, ideas and information on what's new. In particular, I'd like to say a huge thanks to Prabhakaran Andiappan, Corrine Roucou and Mike Camp who went out of their way to help out.

Acknowledgements

Cover photograph: Sheikh Zayed Grand Mosque, Matteo Colombo/AWL ©
Photographs pp26-7 (clockwise from top left): Trabantos/Shutterstock ©; Urbanmyth/Alamy Stock Photo ©; Elena Bee/Shutterstock ©; Torsten Bahr/500PX/Getty Images ©; Monticello/Shutterstock ©.

This Book

This 2nd edition of Lonely Planet's *Pocket Abu Dhabi* guidebook was researched and written by Jessica Lee. The previous edition was written by Jenny Walker. This guidebook was produced by the following:

Destination Editor Lauren Keith

Senior Product Editor Elizabeth Jones

Regional Senior Cartographer Valentina Kremenchutskaya

Product Editors Kate Kiely, William Allen

Book Designer Virginia Moreno

Assisting Editors Andrea Dobbin, Susan Paterson, Alison Ridgway, Sarah Stewart

Cover Researcher Naomi Parker

Thanks to Lindsey Parry, Sasha Drew, Martine Power

Index

See also separate subindexes for:
Eating p157
Drinking p157
Entertainment p158
Shopping p158

Sights 000
Map Pages **000**

Eating

Drinking

Entertainment

Shopping